Karmabusters

Also by Harold Klemp

MAHANTA

This book has been authored by and published under the supervision of the Mahanta, the Living ECK Master, Sri Harold Klemp. It is the Word of ECK.

Karmabusters

Three Spiritual Tools for
Initiates of the Second Circle and above

HAROLD KLEMP

ECKANKAR
Minneapolis
www.Eckankar.org

Karmabusters
Three Spiritual Tools for
Initiates of the Second Circle and above

Copyright © 2007 ECKANKAR

Printed in USA

Library of Congress Catalog Card Number: 2006935556
ISBN: 978-1-57043-236-1

Compiled by Carol Morimitsu and Rhonda Mattern Stapleton
Edited by Patrick Carroll, Joan Klemp, and Anthony Moore
Cover photo by Annette Weihreter-Horn
Text illustrations by Rebecca Lorio

∞ This paper meets the requirements of ANSI/NISO Z39.48-1992 (Permanence of Paper).

Contents

Sri Harold Klemp
the Mahanta, the Living ECK Master

Introduction

The law of life known as the Law of Karma is the great teacher. As you sow, so shall ye reap. It's not a vindictive law; it's a law designed to open the heart to love and understanding.

The Shariyat-Ki-Sugmad, Book Two, reveals, "It is love and love only which will admit the seeker to all the heavenly worlds. . . . If the karma of man has brought him nothing more than a capacity to love, then he has not lived in vain for a thousand past lives."

Why would anyone even want to get rid of karma?

The answer is simple: So that you can open yourself to more love from God. This is the only reason.

The Mahanta, the Living ECK Master shows you many ways to open yourself to more of God's love. And for initiates of the Second Circle and above, chief among them are three spiritual tools to help you resolve your karma.

These "karmabusters" are: (1) initiate reports, (2) your secret word, and (3) the Friday fast.

1

Each chapter of this book covers one karmabuster—how to use it, and how it can help you. The questions and answers that follow reflect light on its many facets.

Use the workbook exercises and tips at the end of each chapter to help make these three spiritual tools part of your life. Later, turn to the Karmabusters Quick Reference Guide in back to review key points.

As you put these karmabusters to use, you will find more divine love, wisdom, and freedom in your life. The only way to stop the tempo of karma is through the spiritual exercises and monthly initiate reports, and to always look to the Mahanta. That is the easy way.

That is how to build a new and exciting life in ECK.

Now let's begin!

Each chapter covers one karmabuster— how to use it, and how it can help you.

The Master's response to her letter, which she had written but not yet mailed, was like the cry of a hawk: a sharp whistle that cut through her self-pity by waking her to a higher state of awareness.

Karmabuster 1
Initiate Reports

Love Letters from the Heart

A fitting title for this could be "Love Letters from the Heart." It is about the monthly initiate report: Do you need to write it or not?

The report is of spiritual service to you. Karma is a very real factor in life, but few people outside the ranks of ECKANKAR have a way to deal with it successfully. So they end up victims of life. As an ECK initiate, you have the special privilege of putting your thoughts, hopes, dreams, burdens, and fears down on paper and thus release them with the help of the Mahanta, the Living ECK Master.

The initiate report is about surrender. In turning over your concerns to the Master, you give up their hold on you. Usually, such cares only produce fear, doubt, and unhappiness. They are not worth the bother.

Your monthly report is but one of several ways to take advantage of the ECK force and drop habits or other faults that chain you to the lower worlds. Some people like misery. If anyone in ECK is of

The initiate report is about surrender. In turning over your concerns to the Master, you give up their hold on you.

5

that mind, it would be better to search for another path to God, because it shows a weak desire for the realization of God. Other ways the Mahanta helps an individual shed useless karma are in dreams, in contemplation, and in daily life. The initiate report is thus one of several aids to help you reach a better and more happy place in life.

How important is your initiate report?

What do you say in the report?

And do you need to put it in the mail?

The initiate report is one of several aids to help you reach a better and more happy place in life.

How important is it? Some Higher Initiates feel they are above writing a report to the Master because they are done with karma and its effects. That is half true. The Fifth Initiation does allow an individual to call the Soul Plane home here and now, but the fact remains that earth is still a person's base of operation until he sheds the human body. In the meantime, it's life as usual.

Even High Initiates need to deal with problems. Just because many ECK initiates are further along spiritually in this life than even the early saints, the battle with the negative forces won't end until they leave the lower worlds for good. At the very least, High Initiates find daily karma as much a challenge as does any other ECK initiate. But the Mahdis and higher are done with most past-life and reserve karma.

So the initiate report can help everyone in ECKANKAR. No one is too big, too wise, or too important to omit this spiritual discipline.

What to say in an initiate report?

Some give an inventory of dreams, insights, and other experiences—or even a simple plea for help. The simplest letter ever sent to me had two words besides the author's name: "Mahanta, help!"

Other people tell about the miracles of ECK, such as a gift of healing. Still others give insights into a recent ECK initiation and tell how life is different from before. A chela might speak about a discourse. Such was the case of the woman who caught a glimmer of truth from a *Letters of Light & Sound 1* discourse on sin, spiritual law, and karma. Others ask for spiritual aid.

And finally, does the report actually need to go into the mailbox?

Ask the Master in contemplation. You need not always put a report into writing, for it may serve as well to form a letter in your mind and imagine sending it to the Mahanta, the Living ECK Master. A good time to do that is on the last Friday of the month.

Some chelas say they are too busy to bother with even an inner report. It's their loss. Maybe if they took the time to keep their inner lines of communication open to the Master, they would find ample time to fit everything in. People are often in a rush simply because they don't make time for the Mahanta.

By the way, the Wisdom Notes in the *Mystic World* are my "Love Letters from the Heart" to you.

The simplest letter ever sent to me had two words besides the author's name: "Mahanta, help!"

Help with Karma

How can the simple act of writing an initiate report to the Master affect my karma?

It's a very direct method of removing the curtain between cause and effect in your own life. This curtain is called lack of awareness, or ignorance. When it's gone, you have a much clearer view of your behavior and the effects of it.

You must first recognize your part in a karmic matter before the ECK will begin to adjust the karma involved.

One good way of formulating your problem or situation is in the monthly report. When you sit down to write a report, it helps you gain a spiritual overview of your questions. Once you see your responsibility in a matter, you will unfold much faster as Spirit goes about fixing the problem.

Thus you can work out much of the karma you have through your initiate report. It will also remind you of things that have happened in the dream state, which is another place to work off karma and move forward on the path to God.

How does recognizing my problems help to cure them?

Spirit knows our problems and our situations, but It won't heal or cure them until we have come to an understanding of what they are and can put our finger on exactly what is wrong in our life. As soon as we can do that, the ECK begins to work.

It is our attitudes that have caused karma. Thus you can see that as quickly as we can identify and let go of those attitudes that harm us, we will move smoothly into the spiritual worlds.

An attitude of the loving heart can dissolve

You must first recognize your part in a karmic matter before the ECK will begin to adjust the karma involved.

much of the unnecessary karma. It becomes pow-
erless to touch us because of the protection of the
Mahanta.

**In writing an initiate report, can I actually heal
karma from a past life? If so, what are some
ways such a healing could show up in my
present life?**

The process of writing uncovers our own
deepest thoughts and emotions. As you transcend
the daily reality, it's found to be a mask that covers
old feelings, old fears. We can change the future
through an understanding and reconciliation of
the past.

As a child, a certain ECK initiate I'll call Sally
had problems with her right foot and leg that
ranged from sprains to serious injuries. In some
cases, she had even needed surgery. Today, mar-
ried and working as a secretary, she finds her old
nemesis of a weakened limb returning to make
life as a wage earner more difficult. She recently
sprained her right ankle again. To cheer her up,
her husband brought home an orchid with nine
flowers in full bloom.

An hour before dinner, Sally had finished her
monthly initiate report to the Mahanta. The report
allows the free use of imagination, to view life
from every angle and then try to sort the problems
into some order. Sally used her imagination to
detail her frustration with work and the distress
that her sprained ankle was causing.

After dinner that evening, she and her husband drew their chairs close to the orchid to

*We can
change
the future
through an
understanding
and
reconciliation
of the past.*

do their daily ECK spiritual exercise. As they admired the plant, tears began to well up in Sally's eyes. The word *defective* kept coming to mind. She felt defective in her own eyes and thought that the Mahanta and SUGMAD saw her that way too. The couple began to sing HU, an ancient name for God, a simple yet beautiful song of prayer.

Her state of awareness began to open to a past life. Born somewhere in the Middle East, she was then a boy with a clubfoot and a deformed right leg—the same side as her pain in this lifetime. Her family in that life had left her in the desert to perish. However, a caravan came along to rescue her, only to enslave her in cruel surroundings. Sally recalled that past life as one of pain and severe hardship, for her rescuers treated her like a defective human being.

Those strong feelings of being defective carried over into the present life.

They also accounted for her feelings at work, where she thought of herself as only a secretary, doing menial work. It made her angry and impatient with her employer. The sense of being a slave nearly crushed her spirit at times.

Two days after she wrote her spiritual report to the Mahanta, her ankle began to heal at last.

Two days after she wrote her spiritual report to the Mahanta, in which she had asked to understand her feelings of inferiority, her ankle began to heal at last. Then also came a recognition of the spiritual value of her secretarial duties at work. They were giving her strength for the next portion of her journey home to God.

The Master's response to her letter, which she had written but not yet mailed, was like the cry of a hawk: a sharp whistle that cut through her self-pity by waking her to a higher state of awareness. He had let her see a past life. It gave meaning to what felt like undue pain and drudgery in the present.

Moreover, it was the gift of the orchid that had opened her heart, for healings occur easiest in an atmosphere of love.

Use imagination in your initiate reports, dreams, and contemplations, for the Master's hawk appears to those who live by the precept "I can imagine, therefore I can be more."

How do you solve a matter of healing when a chela writes you with a request?

The problem is turned over to Divine Spirit, which goes to work immediately, even before your letter reaches its destination. I do nothing of myself, but it is my responsibility and spiritual duty to act as an instrument for the spiritual power to flow out to all and help anyone who makes a request.

I cannot tell if a person's request will be fulfilled as he desires. Spirit will use Its own divine wisdom to help each one for his individual welfare. It may guide him to the proper medical doctor or in some other way address Itself to the condition behind the problem.

If the chela will surrender all of the problem to the Mahanta, the Inner Master, the problem will be taken care of in due time.

The problem is turned over to Divine Spirit, which will use Its own divine wisdom to help each one for his individual welfare.

Can you share some other ways healing may come when I write to the Master?

A woman who was going through a very troubled time in her life sat down one morning to figure out what to do about it. The idea came to her to write an initiate report. When things get too heavy, this invites Divine Spirit to begin working them out.

But as she began to write about her situation, she became so depressed that she couldn't finish the letter. Laying down the pen, she decided to go into contemplation. She closed her eyes and put her attention on the Mahanta.

The next thing she knew, she was walking on one of the inner planes with the Inner Master, Wah Z. They entered a beautiful Temple of Golden Wisdom.

The next thing she knew, she was walking on one of the inner planes with the Inner Master, Wah Z. They entered a beautiful Temple of Golden Wisdom, and he led her to a room. "This is the Sound room," he explained. "Would you like a Sound healing?"

"Sure," the ECKist said.

He told her to climb up on a large stone table and stretch out on her back. As she lay there, she began to feel the Sound Current of ECK coming through. It felt very soothing, as if all her inner bodies were being massaged. Soon she was calm and relaxed. As the transformation took place, the depression began to leave her.

She came out of the short contemplation feeling completely changed.

The exercise helped her because she had done as much as she could on her own first. The initiate report she had started to write was the trigger that opened her consciousness. She was able to accept the nudge to go into contemplation.

What to Write

How do I start my report? Can I just write down my troubles?

When you write this letter, you're basically opening yourself up to the Inner Master and saying, "I've put my troubles down in front of me. I recognize these as problems, and I would like something to be done about them unless it's karma that is necessary to work off for my own spiritual unfoldment. Then I will accept that too." This is how you go about it.

Is my initiate report to cover other things besides what is troubling me?

You can put down in writing the problems or concerns you have in your daily life. And—*remember this part*—the spiritual benefits that have come to you since you've been a member of ECKANKAR. Or the spiritual experiences, such as Soul Travel, dream experiences, anything that gives you a better spiritual understanding of your life. This is what the initiate reports are for.

These reports are also a way to ask for spiritual guidance, solace, aid, and comfort. They are treated confidentially.

What is the purpose of the monthly initiate report?

The purpose of the initiate report is to give you an overview of the spiritual progress you have

You can put down in writing the problems you have and—the spiritual benefits that have come to you. Or Soul Travel, dream experiences, anything that gives you a better spiritual understanding of your life.

made—or not made—over the past month. Try to assess not only what you have learned since the last report, but what you still need to learn. These letters often describe the events that surround the spiritual principle you have been working with.

The importance of the monthly report is so that you can make a personal assessment: Do I have contact with Spirit? Am I faced with big problems in my life that I'm not able to handle? Write them down.

Do I write only about inner experiences, or is it OK to also write about my daily life?

In your initiate report you can put down whatever is affecting you as well as the other things that I mentioned—such as your dreams and experiences. You make a connection between your outer and your inner life. When you do this, you're going to find help from the ECK.

You make a connection between your outer and your inner life. When you do this, you're going to find help from the ECK.

Can you give suggestions about including dreams from my dream book in my initiate report?

The first rule in keeping a dream book is to write simply. Writing complex ideas in everyday language is hard work. A dream may have so many details in it that you can become sidetracked from the point. To overcome this, write the dream out in full length. Then put it away. At the end of the month, review those inner experiences that stand out. Condense them. Make believe you are an editor on the staff of *Reader's Digest*.

Gather the best of your experiences and revelations, if any, and send them to the Master in your initiate report. It is an easy way to resolve karma.

Should I write even if I feel I haven't made any spiritual progress?

Write from the heart.

Write from the heart. Report exactly what you've seen in your spiritual progress—or lack of it—over the past month.

It helps you define things for yourself spiritually. It also helps me see on the physical if you're keeping up with the spiritual exercises.

Is it possible to write a "wrong" initiate report? In Satsang class, a Higher Initiate recalled a letter that Paul Twitchell once sent him in response to an initiate report. Paul took him to task for too many "personal desires." How much help can I ask for in a monthly report?

Paul's letter was for that Higher Initiate at that time. It does not apply across the board. The Master will sometimes make a sharp point to a chela when gentler means have failed.

You may include anything in your monthly report that comes to mind. Indeed, new chelas often do ask the Mahanta to fulfill personal desires. When they put such feelings on paper, it lets them see their unvarnished thoughts, often for the first time. That process burns away old karma.

And if the Mahanta sees that it will benefit the individual, he may grant the personal desire. It never hurts to ask.

Is there anything that's not appropriate to include in my initiate report?

Initiate reports should contain no funds or administrative matters. Send any donations or communications about ECK membership, discourses, materials, seminars, etc. to the appropriate department at the ECKANKAR Spiritual Center.

How long should my report be?

The initiate report can just be a few lines on a page. It's better if you can keep it to no more than one or two pages. It doesn't have to be very long. It's to help you.

I have a really tough problem that I've been working on for a long time. Can writing my initiate report help me?

So often, people say, "I simply cannot deal with my life. Everything is wrong. I can't get over this problem."

Now this is important: When you're feeling very upset and down on the world, when you don't have the confidence you want or you're feeling at odds with people, this is the time to sit down somewhere and write an initiate report. You don't have to mail it.

The Mahanta works inwardly with each person.

I'm emphasizing this because you'll find that the Mahanta works inwardly with each person. You don't have to understand how it works because that isn't important.

All you have to understand is whether it works for you. If it works for you, that's all that matters because your spiritual unfoldment is at stake here.

Your spiritual freedom and your greater sense of receiving divine love.

First, write down very clearly what's bothering you. Do this in the first or second paragraph. Even the first or second sentence if you can. Say, "This is what's troubling me. I can't handle it." Then keep writing some of the experiences that have happened that support the problem you're having. Say, "I'm having this certain problem with somebody at work. And here are some of the things that this person has done to me."

Write it down. And as you write, after about five, ten, or fifteen minutes, you're going to find that something is lifting from you. You will definitely feel something lifting.

As you write, you're going to find that something is lifting from you.

If it's a really bad problem, you may have to write for fifteen or twenty minutes, not just five or ten. You'll feel something lifting. The problem won't be as heavy as it was before. And if this feeling of depression comes back again—in a day or two, a week, or a month—sit down and write about it again. This requires self-discipline.

This is one of the steps to self-mastery: learning how to have the discipline to very directly face what's causing you trouble.

Put it down on a piece of paper. You can do this with a tape recorder too. It doesn't make any difference. Just get it out. Sometimes this will be much more beneficial than seeking professional help.

There's a place for professional counseling. But when you're working with the Mahanta, he can go back beyond birth.

You don't have to worry about childhood traumas. People who worry about childhood traumas forget that everybody comes into this life with a debt. This is responsible for the childhood trauma, not some human being who happened to be thrown into this situation with you in your childhood. That's too shallow.

Any kind of healing that can only go back to your childhood or your birth is a superficial kind of healing. I'm not saying there isn't a place for it. For instance, if you have a toothache, go to a dentist. If you have another medical ailment, go to a doctor. If you can't see well, go to an eye doctor of some sort.

Why? Because you have an immediate physical problem.

But in some of these things, there's a karmic cause way back. Some things you just have to live with, like maybe poor eyesight. But other things you don't have to live with. But you need help that takes you back beyond your childhood.

If you give this over to the Mahanta in an initiate report, he can take you back in the dream state and begin unwinding this karma.

If you give this over to the Mahanta in an initiate report, he can take you back in the dream state and begin unwinding this karma.

No one else can do that for you.

This is when you're going to be unwinding the real cause of the serious problems that are making you the flawed spiritual being that you are today, but which you do not have to remain.

You mentioned forming my report in my mind. Can I combine this with a spiritual exercise to help me get answers to questions and become more aware of the Inner Master?

The Easy Way technique is an opportunity for learning to rely on the Inner Master. Mentally ask your question while you're doing the Easy Way technique, and again ask it before dropping off to sleep at night. The answer will come, sometimes in an obvious manner. Other times it comes subtly—through the advice of a friend, a humorous anecdote, or as a symbolic dream that you develop the knack of interpreting for yourself.

List all your questions on a sheet of paper. A month later, review them to see if any have resolved themselves. Do this with all your questions every month, and send me a report, if you like, regarding the results.

Mentally ask your question while doing the Easy Way technique, and again before sleep. The answer will come, sometimes in an obvious manner, other times subtly.

I am depressed over the condition I find my life in. Can my initiate reports help me make changes in my life?

Sit down and list the things you like and do not like about yourself, in separate columns. Look at them once a month when you write your initiate report. Look back over the past thirty days for any changes the ECK has brought to you.

Self-discipline is an absolute necessity if one is to have a productive life in ECK. Replace old tastes and preferences with new, better ones. But do it in the name of the ECK, with love and a sincere heart, or nothing will come of this experiment.

The spiritual exercises build up spiritual momentum for Soul to realize the godlike being that It is; therefore, it is imperative that you do them for a twenty-minute period every day. If you have the discipline for that, I will certainly be with you at all times.

Can chelas write initiate reports if they haven't had the Second Initiation yet?

First Initiates who've had the Dream Initiation and want to write a letter occasionally can do so.

I get letters from people who are not members of ECK too.

Children can also be shown how to send a monthly initiate report. Usually little ones draw pictures.

Can children write initiate reports?

Children usually have a more direct link with the Mahanta than many adults do. They do appreciate, once or twice a month, the chance to participate with reading the ECK discourses. For example, ask them, Would you like to read ECK tonight? They can also be shown how to send a monthly initiate report. Usually little ones draw pictures.

Mailing Your Reports

When should I mail my reports?

If you feel you don't have contact with the Inner Master, then write an initiate report and send it to me. If you are having contact with the Light and Sound and the Inner Master, write the initiate report anyway; but you don't have to mail it. It's simply for your own benefit to see what has happened during the last month.

Where should I mail my report?

If you mail your report, address it to Sri Harold Klemp, PO Box 2000, Chanhassen, MN 55317-2000 USA.

You can write *IR* or *IRO*—which stands for *Initiate Report Only*—at the bottom left-hand corner of the envelope. It helps in the mail sorting at the ECKANKAR Spiritual Center. It helps me to get through my work a little faster.

I feel I do have contact with the Inner Master. After I write my report, what do I do with it?

If you have inner contact with the Mahanta, then you don't have to mail it. You can put it on your dresser, next to your bed, or in a drawer. But if you're in any doubt, feel free to send it to me.

Reading Reports

You helped read initiate reports before you were the Living ECK Master. So do you have others help you now? Is it OK for me to write about confidential matters in my report?

Put anything at all in your initiate report that is of spiritual concern to you. Each report is treated with the greatest confidentiality.

Each report is treated with the greatest confidentiality.

I ask a handful of selected Higher Initiates to help me with the initiate reports. They are, in effect, acting under my direction like special ECK Spiritual Aides (ESAs). Every report is read in confidence with divine love.

In this respect, each selected H.I. has the same obligation as a doctor or a member of the clergy does. Later, they are to forget the details.

They help me overcome the physical limitations of time and space so that I am able to serve you better.

How do you find the time to read the initiate reports you receive?

The initiate reports are so important I have them sorted into categories. I ask to see a certain category of problems, or certain spiritual experiences. The stack of mail from initiates is just one bit of the mail I handle, and I have to get administrative help as I've mentioned. Otherwise I couldn't deal with more than a hundred chelas in this lifetime.

But the people who are reading them are very carefully selected. No one outside the circle knows who's doing it. I haven't found a breach yet. They are instructed carefully in the sacredness of the communication between the initiate and the Master. To me it's such a trust that if someone violates it, it's a matter for firing. I feel very strongly about it.

Your reports come to my desk regularly. Sometimes I want to write and say, "Yes, your letters are read." But you know that already.

Know that every letter you write to the Mahanta is answered immediately on the inner, whether or not you choose to mail it.

I read many of these letters physically. I read all of them the other way.

Will I get a response?

Because of the volume of mail I receive, I seldom send a written response. However, know that every letter you write to the Mahanta is answered immediately on the inner, whether or not you choose to mail it.

There are many letters that come across my desk—letters from the happy, the ill, the young, the brokenhearted. As the Inner Master I can be with each individual in the hour of greatest joy or need.

You may hold inner conversations with me, if you like, because in Soul body I am always with you. A deep love for life is what carries one eventually into the Ocean of Love and Mercy. Love attracts love, and all the spiritual blessings of the SUGMAD are given unto you.

More Gifts from Initiate Reports

Please share with me the spiritual reason for initiate reports.

Writing the report, no matter how brief, is like an expression of love. Gratitude for the good things that the ECK has already given us keeps our relationship with the Mahanta open and warm.

When one sends an initiate report, it is an act of spiritual surrender—of attachments to old ideas, etc. As with money, so with initiate reports—lend no more than you can afford to lose. The reports are to give chelas the opportunity to unload their mental, emotional, and spiritual burdens.

It is up to each person how much he wishes to gain from my offer. No one is forced to write an initiate report.

It is up to each person how much he wishes to gain from my offer. No one is forced to write an initiate report.

If the Mahanta knows my problems already, why is it important to write them down in an initiate report?

The initiate report is for you. It is a love gift from the Mahanta, to help you clear the hurdles of life. The report is a privilege. Many new chelas in ECKANKAR take advantage of it; later they write less often, until finally, not at all. They feel the reports are a burden to the Master. But let him worry about that. If there is a need, or even when your life is running smoothly, drop a note to him about your progress.

I'm grateful the initiate reports allow me to release my burdens. Are there other benefits?

I have heard people complain to me, "I'm just not having any spiritual experiences." And yet the same people have just told me, within the past year, about two or three outstanding Soul Travel or dream experiences. At the time, they understood perfectly the significance of the experience and they were so grateful.

But the human mind has a habit of forgetfulness. Three or four months go by, and they don't remember anything. They then say, "Well, I'm not having any experiences in ECK at all, nor have I ever."

I remember, they forget. This is why I say it would be nice if you wrote these things down. It would save me a lot of correspondence.

For myself, I found the monthly initiate reports to be exceedingly helpful to recall the inner experiences that I'd had during the month. This holds true whether a person mails them or not. If you have a good linkup with the Inner Master, it's not necessary to mail the monthly initiate reports; but you may find it helpful to write them for your own use so that you can look back and see what

I found the monthly initiate reports to be exceedingly helpful to recall the inner experiences that I'd had during the month.

has happened, if anything, whether on the inner or the outer.

Is there some greater purpose for remembering and writing down our spiritual experiences in our initiate reports?

You may miss the connection at first between the mission of the Living ECK Master and the life of Portugal's Henry the Navigator, of the early fifteenth century. Henry actually set up the conditions that enabled Columbus to discover America.

Until Henry's day, sea charts were closely guarded secrets. Many of them reflected errors of the clergy, whose maps tried to rest upon their understanding of the Bible. Henry changed all that.

Portugal became a country committed to exploration. Henry required the sailors to debrief after each voyage. Every bit of new travel information was incorporated into maps that marked latitude and longitude. Slowly, Portuguese sailors pushed back the walls of ignorance that enclosed the world then.

That's what the Living ECK Master is doing today: The sailors of the cosmic sea are recording their journeys into the unknown world beyond the physical plane.

This is the purpose of their spiritual journals, their initiate reports, and the books and articles they write. We must compile this information in the interest of spiritual survival. Many hands will contribute to this mission as best they can.

Do you see?

The sailors of the cosmic sea are recording their journeys into the unknown world beyond the physical plane.

How important are my initiate reports and other spiritual disciplines in gaining initiations? In experiencing Self- and God-Realization?

I greatly appreciate your letter and the service you give to bring the ECK message to the uninitiated. All that's important is that the initiate undertake the self-discipline to write a monthly report concerning his spiritual affairs.

One gains inner initiations through the spiritual unfoldment that comes with regular practice of the spiritual exercises. To receive outer initiations, however, the completion and balance for those of the inner, one must keep up the outer membership and study of the ECK discourses. The inner initiations are not complete without the outer ones.

Not everyone will have vivid inner experiences but will instead see Divine Spirit working in their daily affairs.

The sincere initiate, who wants the experience of Self- and God-Realization, must also begin to work with one of the Friday fasts mentioned in chapter three. Not everyone will have vivid inner experiences but will instead see Divine Spirit working in their daily affairs.

Workbook

Initiate Reports and You

1. What especially caught your interest in this chapter?

2. As you read the questions and answers in this chapter, did another question come to you? You can take a moment right now to write to the Mahanta about it in a short initiate report.

3. Are you working on a challenge in your life or are you concerned about something? Pause for a moment, and write from your heart to the Master, surrendering it to the ECK. Or you can form the initiate report in your mind and imagine sending it to the Master.

   What did you notice?

4. What gift from initiate reports stands out for you? Take a moment to express your gratitude to the Mahanta in a little thank-you note. Then open yourself to his response. You can write this down as well, if you wish.

Ready to Write Your Monthly Initiate Report?

1. Choose a day to write your initiate report this month. Date: _____
(If you get the nudge to write your report sooner, go ahead and write.)

2. Here are some topics you can include in your report from "What to Write", pp. 13–20. You can check the topics you'd like to write about, and add your own insights from the Mahanta on what to include.

____ Spiritual experiences, Soul Travel and dream experiences

____ Insights, thoughts, hopes, fears

____ Problems, concerns

____ Your spiritual progress—or areas to improve

____ A plea for help or spiritual aid

____ Your gratitude for the miracles of ECK, such as gifts of healing or the presence of the Mahanta

____ Insights into a recent ECK initiation

____ What you have gained from an ECK discourse

____ Other:

3. On your calendar, you can mark one day each month to set aside time for writing an initiate report and for reviewing this chapter.

4. Before writing your report, ask the Mahanta what you should write about—what is best for your spiritual unfoldment at this time? After writing your initiate report, what do you notice? You can jot down your insights here.

Your secret word opens the channel between you and the
Master so I can give you the secret teachings.

Karmabuster 2
Your Secret Word

Entering a New
Arena of Consciousness

*O*ccasionally, some of you want guidance in receiving a secret or new word for the Third Initiation or beyond. Here are some tips to keep in mind.

Everything centers upon your awareness of the worlds inside you.

This awareness, in turn, depends fully upon your discipline in doing the Spiritual Exercises of ECK—daily. Then, your next spiritual step is assured. A secret word is like leaven. It fits your vibrations, which rise only with the loving, diligent practice of the Spiritual Exercises of ECK.

Can it be any more clear than that?

Someone at the Second Initiation receives his personal word from the Mahanta, as do ECK initiates of all circles. But through the Initiator. Beyond the Second, however, the responsibility shifts to the candidate to make the inner connection with the Mahanta and receive the secret word directly.

A secret word is like leaven. It fits your vibrations, which rise only with the loving, diligent practice of the Spiritual Exercises of ECK.

The Mahanta gives you a new word in the hidden recesses of your heart. For that reason alone, your mantra is truly a *secret* word, and it complements your inner and outer sides in the fullest measure.

Your personal word is a master key to the golden kingdom of heaven.

The Third Initiation opens the gate to your free coming and going to certain regions of the Causal Plane, the region of first causes. This level of consciousness deals with cause and effect, as well as with past lives. Yet as a new Third, you're ready to accept only some of the knowledge that is available with respect to the many interplays of the Law of Resonance in storage there.

So at some point during the Third Initiation, the Mahanta comes to offer you another master key.

This new secret word allows access to fresh areas on the Causal Plane for exploration. Your daily practice of the spiritual exercises has prepared you for a deeper understanding of the human and divine forces that have shaped your unfoldment during countless past lives.

Thus, you may receive more than one new word during the Third Initiation. Each new word signals a mini-initiation.

Further inner initiations within a major outer one holds true for all levels, from the Second through the Eighth, and even higher. In any case, the Master gives such opportunities to all who prove worthy of the secret knowledge.

From all this, you grow in love, wisdom, and

Your personal word is a master key to the golden kingdom of heaven.

understanding. And compassion.

What signs may foretell your readiness to enter a new arena of consciousness? Pay close attention to any dream or Soul Travel experience that treats, say, a wedding or a graduation ceremony.

A wedding celebration in the dream states often marks the union of Soul and the ECK, Holy Spirit. It signifies a linkup with the Sound Current. So take note. Look for a confirmation experience, or a series of them, to follow. Likely as not, it was an inner initiation.

What signs may foretell your readiness to enter a new arena of consciousness?

A graduation ceremony differs a bit in its approach. Here, the Inner Master calls forth the fact of a successfully completed term of instruction. Graduation means you qualify for new opportunities. Like an initiation.

So graduations or weddings are a key indicator.

Yet other dreams besides those dealing with a graduation or wedding may foretell another inner ECK initiation within one's major outer initiation.

You may awaken from a dream with a vivid recall of having had a conversation with someone. That individual often gives no indication of being an ECK Master, but the meeting leaves you within an aura of love and goodwill. Look for further confirmation in later contemplations or dreams.

You will know a confirmation when it occurs.

Again, you may awaken in the other worlds to the delightful peace of a garden, ocean beach, or mountain retreat. Alone or in another's company. It, too, may indicate you've moved to a higher place of spiritual living.

So how might a new word come to you?

The ways are beyond number.

But, by way of example, an official at a graduation ceremony may hand you a rolled-up scroll. You unwind it. On the parchment inside you find one word or several words penned in an elegant script. Chances are, it's your new mantra.

How is a new word confirmed?

You must try it. Often you feel a sense of loss in abandoning your old word, for it has served you well, becoming a sure, trusted friend over the weeks and months.

Let go of the old; take hold of the new.

A reminder: your major ECK initiations—the Second, Third, and up through the Eighth—receive a written confirmation from the ECKANKAR Spiritual Center. The minor inner ones within a major outer one do not.

About the Secret Word

The whole key to the secret worlds lies in the initiate's personal word and his creative use of it.

What happens inwardly when I chant my secret word?

In ECK, the initiate goes inward and does something. Chanting the secret word imparted to him during the initiation, he contemplates on the Sound and Light, and the form of the Living ECK Master. Upon meeting the Inner Master, the initiate is taken to the inner temple and there partakes of the Audible Life Stream of ECK.

The whole key to the secret worlds lies in the initiate's personal word and his creative use of it.

The Shariyat-Ki-Sugmad, Book One, offers this:

To utter the Word, or the ECK mantra, in a special arrangement, is to build one's own future in the other worlds. This is especially true of building in the Akasha, the primal matter force. The ECK enters into the composition of all beings and things of life. It is the primary Sound of every world within the universes of the Sugmad. The sounds of the oceans, the whistling of the winds, the rustle of trees in the forests, the beating of drums, the noises of great cities, the cries of animals, and the words and emotional sounds of people are the natural elemental sounds of the ECK.

Help with Karma

How does chanting my secret word help me with karma in my life?

This word unlocks the Master power—the ECK. It doesn't control a situation. If something is not going very well at work, you don't begin singing this word to yourself in order to control your boss so he'll get off your back. Maybe the guy wants to fire you, and you're trying to figure out how to stay there because you need the paycheck to eat and live. So you work with it in a different way.

You say, I turn this situation over to Spirit so when I have learned the lessons that are necessary for me to understand another divine principle, then this burden can be taken from me.

This is how one's secret word works. Each person has his own.

You say, I turn this situation over to Spirit so when I have learned the lessons that are necessary then this burden can be taken from me.

Once I turn a problem over to the ECK, what happens?

The spiritual exercises open a direct line to the ECK. The secret word expands the consciousness so that we can grasp solutions already at hand. Once you catch the knack of getting insight from the essence of God, then you are free to examine and study everything in life to your heart's content.

Can chanting my secret word help me get rid of karma caused by the five passions of the mind?

The power of Soul is ignited by the chanting of your word.

The path of ECK doesn't eliminate the five passions of the mind; we learn how to control them. How? By focused attention, the power of Soul, which is ignited by the chanting of your word.

By chanting your word, you instantly have the power to raise yourself in consciousness to the point where you are able to step back from any situation so it doesn't overwhelm you. Then you can look back at it objectively and unemotionally, and figure out what's happening.

How can I remember to sing my secret word and sidestep karmic situations?

There's always something around trying to get us into trouble. Sometimes it is our mind, sometimes it is other people. Yet whatever the irritation, a chela of ECK must have the self-discipline to sing his personal word or HU. This lets him elude any trap set by another.

In the end, lack of awareness always causes grief. The use of our secret word must become second nature, so we sing it the moment something disturbs us. Singing it is a self-discipline. It, in turn, gives us self-direction, which means a greater amount of spiritual freedom.

If I chant my secret word, will all my daily burdens be lifted?

We squeeze what we can out of life. We do it through the ability to tune in to Divine Spirit, or the ECK, by chanting our sacred word. This is how we come in contact with It.

Not that God lifts our difficulties and our burdens, but God shows us the way to get through them while learning the lessons needed to give us strength. In this way, we become strong enough to walk the road that takes us back home to God.

So when you ask me as the Living ECK Master to take your burdens, I can walk beside you and help you, but I won't carry your burdens forever. Gradually, as you get stronger, there comes a time when I give more and more back to you.

As *The ECK Satsang Discourses*, Third Series, says:

> No one should sit back, expecting his consciousness to be changed for him. He must play an active part in life; and the use of his personal mantra, if he is a chela, becomes the force which—with the Mahanta—guides him to active spiritual progress.

The use of our secret word must become second nature, so we sing it the moment something disturbs us.

If chelas don't use their secret word in the Second, Third, or Fourth Initiations, will they have a big ball of karma to work off as Fifth Initiates?

People who don't use their secret word might never become Fifth Initiates.

Some initiates are lazy. They shortchange their own unfoldment by not using their secret word or doing the Spiritual Exercises of ECK. Yet they appear to move ahead through the initiations like everyone else.

But how are they different?

First, they have serious problems with others in the ECK community. Second, often they refuse to support the Mahanta, the Living ECK Master. Third, they are unhappy.

What's it all about?

Their lazy past has caught up with them, and suddenly they are out of harmony with ECK. Like an untuned violin. Although some reach the Fifth Circle, they begin to have more and more problems in ECK. They believe they have fooled the ECK, the Mahanta, and others, but it all catches up with them.

A Fifth Initiate has worked off fate and reserve karma, but a lack of spiritual discipline during the earlier ECK initiations will begin to show up on the Fifth Level as bad habits. These make too much daily karma. Some Higher Initiates create so much of it that they won't work it out in this lifetime, so it spills over into their file of reserve karma.

In short, they have slid backward in their

People who don't use their secret word are like an untuned violin.

spiritual life. Some will lose outer initiations, and a few even try to leave ECK.

You win heaven daily with your secret word.

I don't seem to have experiences when I chant my secret word. Could I be doing something wrong? What should I be watching for?

Please do not become discouraged by your apparent inability to have any experiences during contemplation. The secret word is like a spiritual vitamin that builds one's inner strength over a certain length of time.

Deep changes occur in you when you chant your word. Karma is dissolved from the lower bodies until the weight on Soul is lightened. Then, when you are most relaxed in the serenity of the Mahanta's abiding presence, he will take you into the Sound and Light of God—which is your main goal at the time.

In due course, you should find yourself suddenly in a new and joyful inner state that will prove to you once and for all that you are Soul, a spark of the SUGMAD.

Deep changes occur in you when you chant your word. Karma is dissolved from the lower bodies until the weight on Soul is lightened.

Using Your Secret Word

Where does the special power of my secret word come from?

The personal mantra has no power but by the Mahanta. The secret word fits the individual's rate of vibration and is the tuning fork that puts him in tune. The ECK is one and the same, but each Soul is at a different level of consciousness. The word attunes one to the ECK.

For more insights, contemplate on this passage from *The Shariyat-Ki-Sugmad*, Book One:

> A personal mantra, the secret word which fits each initiate, is an instrument for linking up with the ECK. With its sound it brings forth its content into a state of immediate reality. The Word is the ECK power, not merely speech. The mind can neither evade nor contradict it and will often wrestle to keep from accepting it. But whatever the Word expresses, by its very sound it exists—and will come to pass in each of those who use it. The Word is action, a deed immediately calling forth reality. It is not merely a sound, but an action of the ECK in motion upon whatever plane the initiate is performing.

How do I use my secret word?

You use your word by chanting, or singing, it. When in public, at your job, or in a crowd, you can chant it silently.

You use your word by chanting, or singing, it. When in public, at your job, or in a crowd, you can chant it silently. If you are unable to chant silently, you may whisper the word to yourself or think of it. When alone you may sing it aloud, whisper it, or chant it silently.

Spend at least twenty minutes each day doing the spiritual exercises and chanting your word, preferably in the morning upon arising. If you do not have any experience within a half hour, then stop and wait until the next day. If you do experience something, you can continue until the experience is over.

What's the best way to make my secret word a part of my life?

The word you are given during the initiation acts like a key to unlock the protection and spiritual help available from the ECK, or the Mahanta. You chant or sing this word, quietly or out loud, whenever you have need of this help.

For an easy way to make it a part of your life, contemplate this passage from *The Precepts of ECKANKAR*:

> To spiritualize the consciousness, one must take up the secret mantra which is given to him as an initiate and chant it constantly within himself. This opens his consciousness and allows the ECK (Spirit) to enter into him and reactivate that divine spark within himself. Gradually, the initiate's consciousness is broadened until he is able to receive the most complete flow of the ECK that he is capable of as a channel. His body, mind, and consciousness become filled with the Light and Sound of God, and he radiates a beauty that is beyond any comparison.

Gradually, the initiate's consciousness is broadened until he radiates a beauty that is beyond any comparison.

I'm an Arahata, and I also facilitate ECK workshops. Can a group of chelas sing their secret words silently, for example, during a spiritual exercise in a workshop?

A word about chanting in groups: Sing the word *HU*. Recently, an Arahata was to lead a group and decided to have the initiates sing their own word silently. In the class discussion that followed, everything seemed to hover just on the edge of disruption. Through this experience, she recognized the power of the secret word. She now understands its use is solely for one's own contemplation.

Even though her class chanted their secret words silently, it disturbed the group consciousness. HU, on the other hand, smooths it out.

How does using my secret word build spiritual strength in me?

You become so strong that no matter what comes up, you instantly remember to chant your word.

The purpose of the initiation word you use is to create that spiritual foundation where you become so strong that no matter what comes up, you instantly remember to chant your word. All that you are doing is opening yourself to the full help of Spirit that is around you anyway.

What this does is open the floodgates of your understanding.

On this subject, *The Shariyat-Ki-Sugmad*, Book One, says:

> The experiences of Soul in realization of Itself and Its mission can only be acquired under the guidance of the Living ECK Master and by constant practice. After such preparation, the individual secret word is used and all the accumulated forces of Its incarnations are aroused in the initiate. This produces the conditions and power for which the word is intended. The uninitiated may utter any specific word or mantra as often as he likes, but it will not produce anything for him.
>
> The secret of the special individual word

for each initiate is something not intention-
ally hidden. But it has been acquired by self-
discipline, concentration, inner experience, and
insight. Like everything of value and every form
of spiritual knowledge, it cannot be gained
without effort. In this sense it is like profound
wisdom that does not reveal itself at first glance
because it is not a matter of surface knowledge,
but a deep realization of the inner self.

I wonder if I'm saying my new secret word the right way. Is there a way to tell?

This example may give you some ideas on how
to get your answer.

An ECKist in Japan got his Third Initiation. He
tried the secret word as soon as he got home, but
it didn't work. It was the right word, but since he
didn't know how to pronounce it correctly, he
didn't realize it was right.

About a week later, while riding on the subway, he began to compose his initiate report in his
head. It was his habit to form it in his mind before
he wrote it down and sent it to the Living ECK
Master. As usual, he mentally reviewed his spiritual progress and the experiences he'd had—or
not had—in dreams and in Soul Travel. His attention was still on the ECK when he got off the
subway and headed home.

As he was walking down a deserted street, he
suddenly heard the Mahanta chanting his secret
word for him. This version was given with the
correct pronunciation and the proper accent. It
made all the difference.

As he was walking down a deserted street, he suddenly heard the Mahanta chanting his secret word for him.

Glancing around to make sure no one was nearby, the initiate began to chant the word out loud so he wouldn't forget it. All of a sudden it began to work: He could feel a new awareness coming into him. It was a new wave of ECK, of the higher level of consciousness of the Third Initiation.

Testing Your Word

I just received a new secret word. What can I expect?

Test a word for several weeks. Watch for either subtle changes in attitude brought by the word, or else for direct experiences in the Light and Sound of ECK.

Is there a measure or yardstick to tell if my word is working OK?

If once a month you have a Light-and-Sound experience, that's fine. But better still is being aware of Spirit's help in your daily life.

If once a month you have a Light-and-Sound experience, see the Inner Master, or have an inner experience that you know is spiritual, that's fine. You actually are having many more experiences than you recall. I want you to remember at least one a month to keep your confidence up. But better still is being aware of Spirit's help in your daily life.

Can you share a spiritual exercise to help me work with my secret word and gain more confidence in it?

The ECK always brings truth, but truth may come to each of us in different ways. The word, or mantra, you receive at an ECK initiation is your personal key to the ECK Life Stream, but you must experiment with this word.

At first you're apt to think this key is the wrong one, because it seems to open nothing. Work through this initial stage of preparation with a spiritual exercise.

You can use the creative technique that follows:

Chant your secret word and imagine it emblazoned upon a golden key. Fit this key into the lock of a door. Swing open the door. There, do you see? The Light and Sound of God fill the room beyond.

And if that technique should run its course, try a new approach. The key is still OK, but perhaps the lock has frozen. So warm the key with a match or lighter, then insert it into the lock. It will now turn. Also experiment with lubricating oil. But whatever you do, keep working with your imagination and your personal word. Then watch! The Mahanta will feed you new ideas to try.

These exercises develop your creative powers.

In any case, a new spiritual experience of some sort will always turn up. There is always a way. This principle will stand you in good stead with any stalemate. So always look for a way out.

And be assured that your spiritual unfoldment is ever on track.

About Sharing Your Secret Word

I received my Second Initiation. May I share my secret word? Is it the same for the Third Initiation?

Chant your secret word and imagine it emblazoned upon a golden key. Fit this key into the lock of a door.

At the Second Initiation, you are given a secret word of your own by the Initiator. This word supersedes all other words used in the spiritual exercises. You shall not divulge it to others or write it down, even in a letter to the Master. You may share it with your mate if you wish. At the Third Initiation and above, however, the secret word you get from the Mahanta through the inner channels is for you alone, not to share with anyone else.

The Shariyat-Ki-Sugmad, Book One, offers guidance on this spiritual discipline:

> Those who have received a personal secret word from the Mahanta, whether it is through one of the Mahdis (initiates of the Fifth Circle or above) who can give the initiations or from the Mahanta in person (outwardly or inwardly), shall never reveal their word to another without permission. It brings the spiritual unfoldment of the chela to a halt. He will not have any more advancement until given another secret mantra to replace the other.

When a young child takes the initiation with the family, the parents must decide when the child is old enough to tell him the word.

I'm wondering about my child getting a secret word during his initiation. Is he old enough to understand the importance of keeping it secret?

Children of any age may take the Second Initiation with their parents, who will explain the rite to them when they are old enough to understand the use of the secret word. If you have a baby, the baby can also be initiated.

When a young child takes the initiation with the family, the parents must decide when the child is old enough to tell him the word and explain the importance of the word and how to keep it to himself. This is done in accordance with the family's judgment, not an Initiator's and not someone outside the family circle. The decision is made at home.

At that time you can explain to him the meaning of having the word, how it's used, and how it will help him. You can perhaps use your own personal experience to explain how it has helped you.

Changing Your Secret Word

Does a secret word ever last for more than one initiation?

Sometimes your word will last throughout all the different initiations, from the Second on up; other times it will last for one or two initiations, and then you need a new one.

Sometimes your word will last through all the initiations; other times it will last for one or two, and then you need a new one.

The significance of mantras is found in *The Shariyat-Ki-Sugmad*, Book Two:

> Mantras are ubiquitous in the life of the ECK chela and are used at every significant step in his unfoldment to God. This is the love power which builds for him that great aura of everlasting mercy and compassion. For example: When a chela enters into the ECK Master discipline, the Living ECK Master will sometimes assign him a special mantra for life. This generally occurs at the Second Initiation, and the Living ECK Master is also under an obligation to see that the disciple keeps up this

chant of his special mantra because it constitutes a spiritual link between them. This is one of the reasons why the Living ECK Master always asks for a monthly report, for he can tell if the chela is keeping up his chant through the report as well as other means of spiritual insight.

Would you speak about having a series of spiritual words, not just one? I had the secret word from my Second Initiation for only a few weeks. Ever since, I have been receiving a new word about every six months to a year. I worry that I am not doing something right.

The Master gives a new secret word every time the chela unfolds in awareness.

Your question illustrates how each person in ECK walks a unique path to God Consciousness. The Master gives a new secret word every time the chela unfolds in awareness. The Astral Plane, for example, has many subinitiation levels, and each of them requires a new password for entry. Each new word permits access to a special area of instruction.

The fact that your word changes so often indicates an inquisitive and spiritually adventurous nature.

When should one consider changing his secret word?

One can consider changing his secret word anytime he feels it is not adequate for what he expects. Too many of us, especially the Second Initiates, are locked into the idea that the word is for life. The Mahanta may give a word for life, and when he does, the individual will be directed in its specialized use.

A word given to one during initiation may actually fit the individual for only a few weeks, or it may not have felt comfortable from the start. The point is that fear has no place in the works of ECK since fear is a fixidity of consciousness that is the playground of Kal. It will defeat a person on the path to God every time.

Therefore, use the word from the rite of initiation to fall back upon when your experiments with other words come to no avail.

Why does a secret word or a spiritual exercise appear to stop working?

Anytime a certain exercise no longer works for us, it means we have unfolded beyond the scope of this particular spiritual exercise or personal, secret word.

It's time for us to use our creative abilities to go a step further, to find another word or another spiritual exercise, so that we can tune in to the higher level of spirituality which we have attained in the spiritual worlds. Then it is up to us to become aware of it in the physical state of consciousness.

Anytime a certain exercise no longer works, we have to use our creative abilities to find another word or spiritual exercise.

I feel my secret word isn't working. What happens next?

At a certain time, even during an initiation such as the Second, all of a sudden you may say, It doesn't work for me anymore; what's wrong?

At this point, begin experimenting, like the chemist in his lab. Try combinations—try this word, that word, try different words. Or use the same word that you were given, but try it in different combinations and see if that works.

You begin experimenting.

As you work toward self-mastery, as this Master power—the ECK—flows through you in greater and greater degrees, you've got to make this contact yourself. You are responsible for the disciplines that keep this line open between yourself and Spirit. The key is simple: the Spiritual Exercises of ECK.

If a word works for you, keep going with it. The proof, of course, is if you can see the Light or hear the Sound, or if in the dream state or in contemplation you can see the Inner Master.

Ways to Get a New Secret Word

What's the process for finding a new secret word?

Say you're doing the spiritual exercises, using the word you were given at the Second Initiation. Lo and behold, two weeks pass and the word doesn't work anymore. So what do you do?

You begin working to find another word.

Read *The Shariyat-Ki-Sugmad*, and if you find a word there—perhaps *Anami* or another name which refers to the God realm or the SUGMAD—chant it; try it that night. See how it works.

Try a different word and experiment with it,

> *At this point, begin experimenting, like the chemist in his lab. Try combinations— try this word, that word, try different words.*

because as you go further, more and more responsibility will be given to you for working with
the spiritual exercises and finding a word. The
responsibility rests with you. You have to figure
out how to do it, and there is a way.

If your word has stopped working and you
need another word to carry you through the rest
of your Second, Third, or Fourth Initiation, which-
ever you happen to be in, first go into contemplation. Blank the mind and see which words come
to the forefront of your mental screen.

Let's say the initiation you are in requires a
one-syllable word. See if one of the words or
thoughts or impressions that just happen to come
to you can be reduced to whatever number of
syllables your word had when you were given the
initiation for the particular circle you are in. See
if you can do this. When you find a word, then use
it, try it out, and see if it works.

If it doesn't, wait about a week or two and try
another word, because you are the one who is
going to have to find it. If it still doesn't work, you
can become more earnest with your Friday fasts.
That's what I did.

**Can you give me a specific technique I can use
to find a new word?**

One way to get the word is through the Shariyat
technique. Simply state your problem: I seem to
have outgrown my secret word for now. It no
longer seems to work. I may come back to it later,
but for now I would like to have a new one.

*One way to get
the word is
through the
Shariyat
technique.*

Once you have stated the problem as you see it, forget about it and go on to the next step. Open *The Shariyat* at random, read a paragraph, and contemplate upon what you have read. Then open *The Shariyat* again and read another paragraph. Through the Golden-tongued Wisdom, which is an aspect of the ECK-Vidya, the ancient science of prophecy, the two paragraphs should present some kind of an answer.

What is the easiest way to look for a new secret word?

The most natural way is in contemplation. Ask the Mahanta to give the word that is right for you at this point in your spiritual unfoldment. The problem most have in getting a new word is recognizing the word when it is given to them, for they often reject it as being too plain and ordinary.

Before bedtime, make the request to have a new word, look into the eyes of the Inner Master, and go off to sleep.

The word can also be gotten in the dream state. Before bedtime, make the request to have a new word, look into the eyes of the Inner Master, and go off to sleep.

Another way is to choose a word from your daily reading of the ECK books or discourses. The word may be a symbol, a picture, or even a simple object that is in the kitchen or yard.

How can experimenting help me?

When you do your spiritual exercises, be flexible with them. If one doesn't work for you just the way it's written in an ECK book, try something different with it.

Look for another word. Try out another word. Get it from the inner or go to *A Cosmic Sea of Words: The ECKANKAR Lexicon*, and read until a word seems right. Test it in your next contemplation cycle. If it works, use it. If it doesn't right away, give it a few days, or a month.

Don't get frantic. Look for another word, another spiritual exercise. Invent your own.

Use the spiritual exercises given in the ECK discourses. But then use them to start creating your own so that you can hear the Sound of God and see ITS Light. That's when the maturity of Soul becomes an accomplished fact. Then Soul becomes worthy to step along the path of God and move into the heart of the Ocean of Love and Mercy.

I didn't get a secret word during my Third Initiation. Should I go back to the Initiator for assistance?

In such cases, or if you got a secret word but it no longer works, it is not necessary to go back to the Initiator. This is because ECK is an inner-directed path. Go to the Inner Master instead, and ask for another secret word.

You may have to cast about for the secret word by studying *The Shariyat-Ki-Sugmad*. Find a word in the ECK writings that seems worthy of your highest spiritual aspirations. Or use one of the words found on the Worlds of ECK chart, which is also in *A Cosmic Sea of Words: The ECKANKAR Lexicon* and *Your Road Map to the ECK Teachings*, Volume 2.

Find a word in the ECK writings that seems worthy of your highest spiritual aspirations. Or use one of the words found on the Worlds of ECK chart.

Has my word been given to me, even if I'm not conscious of it?

Something must be said here about how Soul Travel helps one get a word if it does not come during the initiation ceremony. The Mahanta then passes the secret word to the individual during a dream or in contemplation.

You may not remember this word consciously in the physical body, but each time you go into contemplation, it is whispered in your ear or given to you in writing on the inner planes. On each occasion when you go into contemplation and pass a certain point beyond the reach of the conscious mind, the word is again given to you. Later, the repetition of the word finally reaches the outer consciousness. You then remember it and make it an active part of your spiritual exercises.

A certain chela who did not get his word during initiation got it in the manner described above. He had been having a difficult time getting to sleep, so whenever he awoke in the zone between waking and sleeping, he chanted *Wah Z* in order to receive the Mahanta's love. This particular night, in a dream, a scroll appeared in the distance. It zoomed close, and his secret word shone out in a bar of light.

In a dream, a scroll appeared in the distance. It zoomed close, and his secret word shone out in a bar of light.

Unfortunately, he did not commit it to memory before returning to sleep, and it was lost. But the word is always available in contemplation, even though one is not outwardly aware of it.

Some fail to realize that they always have a special, individual word. If the word you have received during initiation quits working, you can always use HU until a new one comes along. One's word offers wisdom, power, and healing equal to one's state of consciousness.

At my Second Initiation, what if I got a different word than the Initiator?

Often when an ECK initiate gets a new word on his own before the initiation and the ECK Initiator gives him another word during the initiation, he wonders which one is right. The one that you receive on your own should always be regarded first, because it comes from your own inner worlds.

But it isn't by mistake or accident that you happen to get two words. Sometimes your own word stops working after a few weeks or months. That's when you use the other one.

Or you can experiment: Try using both words together, or in combination with HU, Wah Z, SUGMAD, or any of the other sacred names in the ECK teachings. As Soul, you can use your God-given creativity—the imaginative power—to invent combinations. The imagination is God's gift to you as a spark of the Divine.

I seem to have gotten my spiritual name on the inner planes. Can you verify this?

One's spiritual name is given at the Ninth Initiation. The name you received is your secret word for the present level of spiritual growth. It is the key that unlocks the powers of the ECK, to lift you into the sublime states of spiritual con-

Your secret word must be kept to yourself or the power of the word will be lost.

sciousness. It must be kept to yourself or the power of the word will be lost.

More Gifts from Your Secret Word

In addition to helping me resolve my karma, how does chanting my secret word help me?

This word is a protective one; it opens the channel between you and the Master so I can give you the secret teachings. It also uplifts Soul so you can Soul Travel. Most of all, it helps you increase your capacity to love.

In this light, you may want to contemplate the following passage from *The Shariyat-Ki-Sugmad,* Book Two:

> Mantra chanting produces a whole series of spiritual effects, mainly that of love. By concentrating the mind on the mantra, a deep sense of peace and love arises just as often as the doer puts himself in any degree of concentration. It is a function which is used to focus the mind to a sharp point that is capable of penetrating through the ordinary thoughts to the deeper layers of Soul which lay beneath.

The word of your initiation level is the starting point to get you into your plane.

Does my secret word help me to have more conscious experiences on the plane corresponding to my level of initiation?

The word of your initiation level is the starting point to get you into your plane; then you begin to experiment with other words in conjunction with your own. In the Second Initiation you are going to be able to explore more than just the

Astral Plane, although there are at least 150 different regions on the Astral Plane, and many of them are highly interesting and enlightening.

For some ECK initiates, using your secret word when you first have an initiation will bring many grand and glorious experiences. For others it won't. This word opens you only to a room.

But as you get established on the plane of your initiation, you can begin chanting another word, perhaps one for the Mental Plane or one of the words you find in *A Cosmic Sea of Words: The ECKANKAR Lexicon*. It's a password that will get you through one of the doors.

Start by chanting your secret word or the ECK word of a plane, then add another word in conjunction with it. For instance, if you want to look at a past life, add the word for the Causal Plane.

Work at this. Try it out for a week or two. If it doesn't work, then try some other word. Keep trying, but in a gentle way. Don't force it. Assume the attitude that someday you know this is going to work—and you just keep trying.

One day on your inner travels, you'll get to a door leading to another plane. The guardian of the door will say, "Yes?" Then you'll say this word to him, and he'll let you into the hallway. From there you'll enter into another room—a whole new spiritual dimension.

This is just one more way to use your secret word.

One day on your inner travels, you'll get to a door leading to another plane. The guardian of the door will say, "Yes?" Then you'll say this word to him, and you'll enter a whole new spiritual dimension.

I've been having nightmares. Can chanting my secret word protect me?

Fear is confronted numerous times within the dreamer's kingdom. One individual found herself lost in the basement of a museum. This image represented the imprisonment of Soul in the material worlds. Finally chancing upon the exit, she emerged from the basement into the outdoors. Instantly a tornado loomed on the horizon, but she choked down her terror by singing her secret word.

A white light, like ball lightning, then swept toward her, causing even more fright than the tornado. As she continued singing her word, she lost her fear of the white ball of light that now blended in smoothly with her aura. The tornado was forgotten.

Surrender to Spirit conquers fear. An inner experience of the sort that she reported builds stamina to meet other trials in day-to-day living.

In a dream, I had left my body and was flying. I was holding a sword that gave me a lot of energy and made me feel like a child. It was guiding me. When I let go of it, it was as though I lost the energy and began falling back toward my body. Eventually I didn't have to hold it anymore, but just had it by my side. What does this mean?

The Mahanta puts energy into your secret word and makes it what it is.

The sword is your mantra, your secret word.

The Mahanta puts energy into your secret word and makes it what it is. Once he establishes this power in your word, one more thing is needed to make it work: your attention. Thereafter this word can lift you into the secret world of dreams. Your secret word connects you with the ECK, the Holy Spirit, which then guides you everywhere. However, should your attention lapse, the dream comes to a swift end and you reenter the body.

With practice, your word becomes so much a part of you that you sing it in time of need without a second thought.

I find my secret word gives me a boost in my dreams. Can HU and my secret word also give me energy to Soul Travel?

The sound of HU, a name for God, is important in your spiritual exercises. The real value of the power of HU is to give Soul the energy to go into the spiritual worlds via Soul Travel, and then begin making Its way home to God. Your personal word is actually a variation of HU that fits your personal vibrations. It's customized to help you in your spiritual unfoldment and in your spiritual exercises.

Your personal word is actually a variation of HU that fits your personal vibrations.

As you do the spiritual exercises and sing HU or your secret word to yourself, that begins a purifying, cleansing action on Soul. Old habit patterns—the gossip, the idle chatter, the dishonesty with oneself—start to fall away.

How does my secret word help me tune in to the ECK and get insights?

Many things happen around you every day which tell you how to live life better and be a channel for God. But it takes awareness to notice them. This is where the initiations of ECK come into play.

Each initiation opens your consciousness a little more, allowing you to see the ways of the ECK more clearly. You gain a greater understanding of how the ECK is using you to serve It; and as you serve It, you get an even greater understanding through direct experience.

The purpose of the secret word is to make a connection, or put you in tune, with the ECK, which is the Holy Spirit. During contemplation, or whenever you are in trouble or want insight into a particular situation, remember to chant your word.

The purpose of the secret word is to put you in tune with the ECK, the Holy Spirit. Whenever you are in trouble or want insight into a situation, remember to chant your word.

I feel like I'm just beginning to understand the power of my secret word. How can I get a deeper understanding of how chanting my secret word transforms me?

Contemplate on these words from *The Shariyat-Ki-Sugmad*, Book One:

> The secret word which the initiate receives during the initiations of the different circles (planes) is not merely sounds to be repeated to oneself, but powerful expressions of the ECK power. Such words do not act of themselves but through the inner self which experiences them. They do not have any power of their own; they are only the means of concentrating already existing forces. They are like a magnifying glass; it contains no heat of its own but concentrates the rays of the sun. It transforms these rays from a mild warmth into a burning heat. The same applies to the secret word of the initiate. His word transforms him from the confused doubtful seeker into the incandescent lover of God.

What is the best way to attune my life with the ECK?

How do you bring yourself into agreement with the ECK, the Voice of God? Make total love for life your one focus. All creation is the handi-work of SUGMAD's love. If you realize this, you will spend the time it takes every day to make this connection with your Creator.

And how can you do that? The Mahanta has brought you a gift too precious. When you sing HU or your secret word, you have a direct line with the ECK, the Voice of God.

When you sing HU or your secret word, you have a direct line with the ECK, the Voice of God.

Service to Life

Can I be a vehicle for the ECK just by chanting my secret word? Does it benefit others as well as myself?

You'll find your answer in this passage from *The Shariyat-Ki-Sugmad*, Book Two:

> To the ordinary man the mantra would ap-pear to be nonsensical, a sound which is only the response of the brain to a certain range of vibration transmitted by the air that surrounds him. But, nevertheless, it is a powerful instru-ment of love and detachment for that ECK chela who practices it regularly. He reaches out to people whom he will never know and changes the course of their lives from the Kal forces which might be gripping them to the ECK which will lead them to God. Few, if any, will ever learn what has happened, but the mantra built up by the ECKist either indi-

vidually or collectively will bring about a change in the worlds; first, that of man and then that of the spiritual heavens where necessary.

I'll give you two examples of how this can play out in an ECK chela's daily life.

A hospital worker was assigned to a patient recovering from a serious operation that left blinding pain, and the patient's immense agony created turmoil in the chela herself. Right away she chanted her secret word. This opened the gates of consciousness so that Spirit could bring healing into the recovery room.

The ECK quickly soothed the patient's torment through miraculous means. This ECKist knows to call upon the Mahanta rather than trying to heal the sick herself, which only causes bad karma through ignorance of the spiritual laws.

Another chela put her secret word to good use while manning a booth at a summer fair. With each silent chant, a person would soon approach the booth to ask about ECK or take an ECK book. "This happened often enough," she said, "that I know now, by keeping my attention on the Inner Master and by chanting my secret word, I make possible the Master's linkup to certain Souls. What a great power and great discovery."

She chanted her secret word. This opened the gates of consciousness so that Spirit could bring healing into the recovery room.

Workbook

Your Secret Word and You

1. Take a moment to open your heart and chant your secret word right now. What do you experience?

2. What do you especially want to remember from this chapter?

3. Here are some of the gifts you can receive from chanting your secret word (from "Help with Karma," pp. 35–39, and "More Gifts from Your Secret Word," pp. 56–61). You can mark the ones that light up for you.

    ____ Increases your capacity to love

    ____ Attunes you to the ECK

    ____ Allows the Master to give you secret teachings and protection

    ____ Helps control passions of the mind

    ____ Uplifts Soul so that you can Soul Travel

    ____ Makes your way easier in life

___ Builds inner strength

___ Opens you to the full help of Divine Spirit

___ Transforms you into a greater spiritual being

4. What other gifts have you experienced?

5. You can express your gratitude for these gifts in a thank-you note to the Master. Then watch and listen for the Master's response to you, his beloved chela. You can write your experience here.

6. Looking for a new spiritual exercise to try with your secret word? Review the sections "Using Your Secret Word," pp. 39–44, and "More Gifts from Your Secret Word," pp. 56–61. You can try one of the exercises as part of your spiritual exercise for today.

7. Wonder if it might be time to change your secret word? You can review "Changing Your Secret Word," pp. 47–50 and "Ways to Get a New Secret Word," pp. 50–56, for information on finding your secret word.

Want to Use Your Secret Word More Often?

1. Ask the Mahanta, What can I do—today—to make my secret word more a part of my life? You can write your answer here.

2. Walk or drive around your neighborhood, silently singing your secret word. Let the Inner Master show you your connection with life around you. What do you experience?

3. Add the following to your daily routine: Read a passage from this chapter before doing your daily spiritual exercises or before going to sleep at night. You may be inspired to chant your secret word during the day.

4. When reading any ECK discourse or book, watch for a passage that especially inspires or interests you. Then pause for a moment and chant your secret word.

5. Ask the Mahanta to show you a passage that stirs your imagination. Then create a spiritual exercise from that passage.

    For example, you can try it with this passage from p. 45: "Chant your secret word and imagine it emblazoned upon a golden key. Fit this key into a lock of a door."

    Then, as a spiritual exercise, imagine a karmic situation in your life as the locked door mentioned above. What happens when you open the door with your key? Write your experience here:

When you are on a spiritual fast you'll find that your attitude and your very words are different. You're not creating karma the way you were before.

Karmabuster 3
The Friday Fast

How to Be the HU

*F*rom time to time it's necessary to speak to you about the Friday fast. What is it? What is the proper way to do it? Why do it at all?

In the early days of ECKANKAR, we used to practice one of three Friday fasts: (1) a water fast for twenty-four hours; (2) a partial fast of fruit, fruit juice, or only one meal for the entire day; or (3) a mental fast. The recommended fast for today is the mental fast. The other two can be harmful to persons with certain health conditions. The mental fast does not need the approval of a physician, and it is the safest and most convenient for anyone to use for spiritual growth.

The path of ECK is the middle path. As such, one need not indulge in excesses of any kind to gain spiritually—and this includes the stress of food fasts.

Here are a few points about fasting in general. The water fast may appeal to people who in past lives liked to wear hair shirts as a sign of

The recommended fast for today is the mental fast. It is the most convenient for anyone to use for spiritual growth.

their love for God. Of course, God does not go in for such odd behavior to express one's love, and the practice of depriving oneself of food often eroded into an act of vanity. The person who could fast longer than others felt it to be a mark of superiority. But SUGMAD has no use for such human pride.

The fruit or fruit-juice fast can harm a diabetic, of course. If I were to insist that an initiate keep that fast—and he couldn't due to medical reasons—would it be right to limit his spiritual growth in such a manner?

But there is the Friday mental fast.

The mental fast is both easy and difficult, much harder than the water or partial fast if done correctly. It means keeping your attention upon the Mahanta all day long on Friday.

There are several ways to do it.

One way is to sing HU inwardly or outwardly. Another way to do the mental fast is to chant your secret word. A third way is to do everything that day in the name of the Mahanta. You may also keep your attention on him, whether or not you're doing anything at all.

But why fast on Friday?

You've heard me say repeatedly that truth builds upon truth. Thus, it may also be that a new spiritual path borrows practices from old religions, updates them, and thus they become an integral part of the new religion. That is what happened to Christianity. It did borrow and alter holidays and ceremonies from pagan religions. In ECKANKAR, and in every other path to God, there is the same regard

The mental fast means keeping your attention upon the Mahanta all day long on Friday. There are several ways to do it.

for what uplifts people spiritually in older paths.

For a while, Paul Twitchell was a Catholic. He saw the value of Friday as a day of special reverence for God, so later he used that day as the basis for the Friday fast in ECKANKAR. The Catholic Church lost something of deep value when it began to downplay its day of fasting. It actually lost the heart of its self-discipline.

It will startle some people in ECKANKAR to think that our fast day is fashioned after that once-familiar day in the Catholic Church. Here again, it takes a spiritual overview to see truth. Where do you think the Catholic Church got the idea? From ECK.

All religions spring from the ECK. Look closely at a religious practice before dismissing it as a superstitious rite. Why let *your* vanity and ignorance show?

The ECK has made all religions. Each path fulfills the inner needs of Souls at a given place in their rise to spiritual freedom.

So what does a special day of fasting do?

So what does a special day of fasting do?

It helps you develop the inner discipline to reach God-Realization. You learn the habit of being in ECK. Every moment. Every day.

Then, when at the bedside of a loved one in critical health, you will remember to sing HU as a way of saying, "I love you." If you are a student in a difficult class on cooking, nursing, or computer science, you will remember to look upon the class instructor as the agent through whom the Mahanta is working. Or should you live in a community where people of a fundamentalist religion shun you, you will remember to call upon the Mahanta. He is always there with the Light and Sound of God to bring you joy.

Yes, the Friday fast is very important for you spiritually. In time, you will find it more easy and natural than ever to be in a high state of being every moment of your life.

Then you will be the HU.

Help with Karma

Is the Friday fast more for spiritual growth than physical cleansing?

It is solely for spiritual growth. It lifts Soul above the social consciousness; it is the easiest way to dissolve past and present life karma.

Are there ways to work out karma without having to go through some of the pain and suffering that normally come as part of life? Is fasting relevant to relieving karmic conditions?

Fasting is one way. It's a discipline. In ECK there are several different kinds of fasts we use. These fasts are done one day a week for twenty-four hours, usually on a Friday.

One is a mental fast, and this can be done in two ways: You can keep your attention on the Inner Master as much as you can, or you can consciously remove every negative thought that comes up. Visualize it being put into the ECK Life Stream where the Light and Sound of God can neutralize it. The mental fast is especially good for

The Friday fast lifts Soul above the social consciousness; it is the easiest way to dissolve past and present life karma.

those who have health concerns and cannot abstain from food.

Although fasting can be beneficial, this doesn't mean you want to go on very long fasts. Nor do you want to go on a fast to change another person's state of consciousness. There are people today who will go on a fast in order to try to bring about a change in consciousness about nuclear power and other things. To fast for the purpose of changing another's state of consciousness is a violation of the spiritual law. You pay for trying to move people from their state of being.

Fasting is very good for working out your own karma. I hesitate to say this because if someone doesn't understand it, he may go on ten-day fasts. He figures if one day is good, ten days is better. Then he starts losing his teeth or developing other imbalances, because he has upset the body's systems.

It's better to do any kind of extended fasting under the direction of a medical doctor, to make sure that your health can stand it. There can be a benefit from it for some, but we are not into asceticism, and most of us do not need such an extreme.

Buddha started out living the life of plenty and then went to starvation and fasting until he was nothing more than skin stretched over a framework of bones. But he found that wasn't it, and he finally came to what he called the Middle Way. Ironically, when he went the middle path, many of his followers left. They thought you had to starve yourself to become spiritual.

The mental fast is especially good for those who have health concerns and cannot abstain from food.

In truth, God really doesn't care what you eat or don't eat.

Can the Friday fast help me with karmic situations in my daily life? How does that work?

If you are having a hard time in your family or at work and you want to get ahead of the game, you can do a Friday fast.

I have found that, when times were especially hard, it helped to do a fast on Tuesday also. Sometimes I would do more than one kind of fast at the same time; keeping the attention on the Mahanta, you can do this. I would do the mental fast at the same time as a partial fast. Then I would sometimes do a water fast on Friday.

At one time somebody was trying to fire me at work. I didn't have money saved and didn't know what to do. So when times were really bad, I would do a juice fast on Tuesday. That used to balance the week out. This was not intended to control anyone else; I merely wanted to purify myself spiritually so that I could get through the situation. But sometimes all kinds of unusual things would start to happen in the lives of those who thought they were attacking me. They began to have so many problems, they didn't have time for me.

The Friday fast is a way to help us pull ourselves, degree by degree, out of our karma.

What the Friday fast does is to start moving you out of the karmic environment in which you find yourself today. Spiritual unfoldment begins where you are today. So the Friday fast is a way to help us pull ourselves, degree by degree, out of our karma. It also helps us develop the ability to handle our problems with much more facility. It's an excellent way to take a step toward our own mastership.

How can doing a mental fast each Friday change me and affect my karma?

Spiritual students are held to account for daily karma.

If a driver speeds seventy-five miles per hour in a fifty-five-mile-per-hour zone and gets caught, there is a fine to pay. No matter how one tries to fool himself that he is above the Law of Karma, the fine must be paid.

The mental fast uplifts the individual's state of consciousness by changing old mental structures and ideas. Thus he treats life with more reverence and looks at it with new eyes.

The mental fast uplifts the individual's state of consciousness by changing old mental structures and ideas.

The mental fast is usually done on Friday. On that day a person thinks and acts in a refined way around others. The fast is a discipline to put one's attention upon the Inner Master. The individual who puts it there is acting in the name of the ECK. This cuts down the daily karma between himself and others.

Why is the mental fast so important to help us achieve our own mastership?

The mental fast is a way to practice the presence of the Master.

Practicing the presence of the Master is an ECK principle that is often forgotten. In times of trouble, some people find it easier to remember the cusswords they learned before coming to

ECK—usually those tried-and-true words that take God's name in vain.

It is quite a discipline to remember to call upon the Inner Master and say, "Mahanta, I need help. If there is some way an individual Soul in the great collection of Souls that live in this world can help, please send that Soul."

Once you become an ECKist, you begin to learn to ask for help. Eventually it becomes second nature.

Further along in ECK you find that you don't specifically have to ask; it is enough to simply recognize that the Master is always with you, and to live with that reality all the time. You look for a way out of the problem, knowing that the ECK, the Holy Spirit, will bring the help when it is needed.

But it will come in a way that also teaches you something about yourself spiritually.

When I do the mental fast and break my regular routine, does this help me rise above the social consciousness? Is this how I work off karma?

When you are on a spiritual fast, you treat people differently at work and at home.

Enlightenment is a gentle thing if it's right, if you're ready for it. It gives you a different viewpoint, a different state of consciousness.

This also occurs when we do a spiritual fast. This is why Fridays have been set aside for you to do a mental fast where you keep your attention on the Inner Master for as much of the day as you can.

You'll notice that when you are on a spiritual fast, you treat people differently at work and at home. You're in a different state of awareness that day. You're pulled out of the routine or rut that the mind likes.

This actually works off karma. The hold of the material world, the attachments, are not as strong on you. This gives you a little more freedom of choice. It puts you in charge of your own life in subtle ways. Other people can feel this.

Sometimes there is something going on at work, something that's not too smooth for you. You can do a spiritual fast for a couple of days. You'll find that your attitude and your very words are different. You're not creating karma the way you were before.

Every thought, word, or deed either purifies or pollutes the body.

Every thought, word, or deed either purifies or pollutes the body.

Now this is very important, very powerful, because you are dealing with states of consciousness. What's coming in is going to go back out there. Then it bounces like an echo; it comes back. So it strengthens and eventually has a very strong influence on you. And this influence can be for either beneficial things or harmful things. The choice is yours.

Most of our problems are self-made. When things go wrong, if we take responsibility and do something that gives us greater understanding, life becomes easier.

This is how it should be, rather than having someone always giving us spiritual, emotional, or physical healings.

Could you explain how keeping my attention on the Master and chanting HU helps me avoid creating negative karma?

When a person takes the Second Initiation, the Mahanta establishes himself at the Spiritual Eye of the person. Chanting HU, the name of God, opens our acceptance of the Mahanta's protection.

All evils and dangers are really caused by our own negative thoughts. Chanting HU neutralizes the negative thoughts that come through the Spiritual Eye. Thus the thoughts are purified and no evil can harm us. Attention on the Inner Master is a great spiritual discipline.

Do my negative thoughts actually make karma?

The Flute of God by Paul Twitchell contains the answers.

In chapter 12, "The Borders of Heaven," you'll find the reason for keeping your focus on the good and desirable, the harmonious and beautiful, to bring it into form. And why it's vital to avoid negative thoughts and words.

These sections show how to move beyond victimhood and turn all your endeavors toward self-mastery.

The Friday fast is for twenty-four hours, which includes while we sleep. Can we create karma in our dreams? If so, how can we avoid it?

Yes, people can create karma in the dream state.

Yes, people can create karma in the dream state. Yet most are unaware that they do so, even as they are unaware of karma they make every day.

Each of us is like a power station. We generate energy all the time, energy that can either build or destroy. If we let unworthy thoughts or desires leave our power station, they pollute everything around us. That is bad karma. Our mind is like a machine, able to issue contaminants around the clock. Our thoughts even run on automatic at night, when we may unconsciously try to control others or harm them in the dream state.

The problem is a lack of spiritual self-discipline.

To avoid making karma, while either awake or asleep, sing the word *HU*. You can do this quietly within yourself or out loud. It's an ancient name for God. Sing it when you are angry, frightened, or alone. HU calms and restores, because it sets your thoughts upon the highest spiritual ideal.

To avoid making karma, while either awake or asleep, sing the word HU.

Ways to Do the Friday Fast

I don't usually fast on Fridays unless I really make myself do it. Is it a necessary part of the ECK disciplines?

Yes, it is. But fasting doesn't have to mean that you go without food and drink only water for twenty-four hours, which is the way many ECKists used to do it.

For most chelas today, I recommend the mental fast. Throughout the day on Fridays, keep your attention on the Inner Master or the Light or Sound in a gentle way. Put a little special attention on the Master or chant HU for as long as you can, even for a few minutes. At first you'll forget and let the attention slip, but gradually thoughts of the Inner Master will come through more and more throughout the day.

You'll find that as you put your attention on the ECK, which is the Inner Master—the higher part of each individual, the inner power, the love current—you are going to deal with people differently.

Your vibrations are different when your attention is on the Master, so people will respond differently to you. Not always kindly, I might add. If a person approaches you in anger, chant HU silently within yourself. This has an amazing effect.

Keep in mind that you're not doing it to change the other person, you're doing it for your own self-protection. It's not like prayer where you say, God, please make him stop. It's more like, God, please give me strength.

If a person approaches you in anger, chant HU silently within yourself. This has an amazing effect.

Why is the mental fast the recommended fast for today?

Food fasts, when taken to the extreme, can destroy the tissues in the body. If you feel there is a good reason to fast, then do it under your doctor's supervision. I have tried just about every fast that you can think of. Sometimes I have helped myself, but more often I've hurt myself.

I recommend that people do the mental fast, where each Friday they keep their thoughts on the Mahanta, the ECK, and the SUGMAD.

I feel that if I'm really serious about my spiritual goals, I should do the water fast—that it's more spiritual. Is this true?

Many years ago someone mentioned the word *balance* to me at a time when I needed to hear it. I was trying all sorts of strange diets, including ten- or twenty-day water fasts. I loved God, I loved the spiritual principle, and I was trying everything I could think of to break through to the divine part of myself.

There are milder fasts we can do. I ask ECK chelas to do one of them once a week. The mental fast—keeping your attention on the Mahanta, the Inner Master, during a twenty-four-hour period—is actually the best for most people. This isn't done in a fixed way where you feel you've lost the entire day if your mind slips off the Master for a second. But every Friday, whenever you remember, simply chant HU or one of the other charged words to put your attention back on the inner reality.

Can a mental fast be as effective as a water fast?

The mental fast is more beneficial for most people than is the twenty-four-hour water fast. Here are some ways to do it: Keep your thoughts upon the Mahanta all day long; throw your negative thoughts into a mental trash can; or ask, How would the Mahanta handle my problems today?

I know I have a lot of past-life karma. Is there a way to do the mental fast to help with this?

If you feel the burden of past-life karma in your life, here's an easy way to resolve a good part of it.

Do all deeds in the name of God or the

Whenever you remember, simply chant HU or one of the other charged words to put your attention back on the inner reality. Or ask, How would the Mahanta handle my problems today?

Mahanta, the Living ECK Master. Let each task hold all your love. Even a humble chore like sweeping the kitchen floor deserves the full span of your love for the Divine Being.

This technique brings love to the fore. An activity performed with divine love burns off karma and affords a spiritual blessing. Often, someone with a creative mind can modify this exercise and develop it as a way to Soul Travel. Listen to the Inner Master.

Karma isn't everything, because neither time nor deeds can measure what love will do. Love is always the trump card. It's the one that determines a lot of things, and it's more powerful than karma.

Karma isn't everything, because neither time nor deeds can measure what love will do. Love is more powerful than karma.

More Gifts from the Friday Fast

How does the mental fast—attention on the ECK and the Mahanta—help my life go more smoothly?

As we go about our day, ideas come through on how to solve problems, how to make our work easier, or how to make things better for someone else.

These ideas come from the creative imagination which, to state it as simply as possible, is God in expression, manifesting Its creation in this world through our actions. This is God speaking through us. The creative imagination is the element that makes us godlike.

By keeping attention on the ECK, the ECKist is uplifted and spiritualized, so that interactions with family, friends, and neighbors ideally are of the highest nature.

I say "ideally," but it's not always practically so, for the road to God-Realization is long and hard. We are constantly being tested to see if, when we face truth, we are found worthy of receiving it.

Can fasting help me remember my dreams?

There are times a block in our spiritual lives prevents us from entering the next spiritual plateau. It is possible to do a fast of some sort to remove this block.

When the dream memory stops for a period of time, efforts in a new direction may be necessary to break through. At one time I would go on a juice fast for a day, then regular food the next day, then juice again for the following day—and alternate between solid food and juices for several days.

But I never did it for too long, since our health is not always able to withstand the strain. This is an individual matter. Not everyone is able to fast physically, and it should always be done with the advice of a physician.

For most chelas I recommend the mental fast on Fridays.

When the dream memory stops for a period of time, efforts in a new direction may be necessary to break through.

Sometimes I feel I have a spiritual block. I have a tough challenge in my life and I can't find a way to deal with it. Can a spiritual fast help with this?

As an ECK chela, when I'd run into a situation where other people appeared impossible to live with—it would've been easy to say, "That person has the problem," and go work somewhere else. But I'd try to work through the problem, if it was at all possible. I would go to extremes to work through it. If I couldn't work it out, I'd change the condition.

When it became more uncomfortable to live with the situation than to fast—when I felt backed into a corner—I would fast. You know the feeling—when you think you just can't take one more day.

I used to do a partial fast to get through these periods. That means a fruit fast, one meal a day, or a mental fast. I always ate enough to carry on with my duties at work, but I'd put my attention on the Mahanta and chant HU. Under really severe conditions I would do this mental fasting every other day.

Usually you can pull yourself through the void with the Spiritual Exercises of ECK. When you're doing a mental fast, you're really doing a spiritual exercise.

Spirit almost drives you through the void if you have the self-discipline to keep going. Spirit gives you the tools to fend for yourself.

Be careful when you do the different fasts. If you have a blood-sugar problem, it's not a good idea to go on a total fast. Today I wouldn't be able to do many of these fasts; my health doesn't allow it. You'll become irritable and tired and cause yourself more problems. You have to use a little common sense when you do these things.

Usually you can pull yourself through the void with the Spiritual Exercises of ECK. Fasting goes hand in hand with the spiritual exercises. When you're doing a mental fast, you're really doing a spiritual exercise.

Why Friday? Is there a mass readjustment of sorts for all ECKists on that day?

Friday is the date established by the Vairagi Order. It has been imitated by other groups in a corrupted form, such as by the Catholic Church in its former days of fish on Friday.

Yes, there is a mass readjustment of sorts for all ECKists on that day.

What are other spiritual benefits of the Friday fast?

The benefits of the Friday fast include self-discipline, giving the body a break by not eating so much, and being in contact with chelas throughout the world since we are all doing it at the same time. It's similar to when you become an initiate of the Second Circle and have an inner communication with other Second Initiates. Some of you are aware of it; others aren't.

The Friday fast is a time designated to put a little attention on the spiritual disciplines.

When we are locked in the human consciousness down here on earth and we have the problems of the five passions that hold us down and keep us miserable and unhappy, we find that the spiritual exercises and the Friday fasts begin to pull us up, little by little.

Occasionally someone asks that a lot of karma be taken off all at once. I usually recommend against it. I've had it taken away fast myself, and it makes a mess. It creates a vacuum in our lives, and then the rest of the karma falls into

The Friday fast is a time designated to put attention on the spiritual disciplines.

the hole where the ECK has suddenly taken a large chunk out.

This is why the ECK Masters often work through the dream state. This allows you to work off some there, work off some here, and it's done in a gradual way so life doesn't cave in on you.

I understand the Friday fast allows me to gradually work off karma—if I have the discipline to do it. How important is discipline in my unfoldment?

We are, in a spiritual sense, going to have to earn our unfoldment in some manner or another. The key to this is contained in the four fundamentals of ECK.

Every ECKist is aware of the spiritual law that everything must be paid for in the true coin. This means that we are, in a spiritual sense, going to have to earn our unfoldment in some manner or another.

The key to this is contained in the four fundamentals of ECK: the first is self-discipline. Then, the absolute inner reliance on the Mahanta. Third, the Spiritual Exercises of ECK; and, finally, the true contemplation of the works of ECK.

Paul Twitchell specifies in *The Spiritual Notebook* that "The ECK Masters did not reach their high state by fleeing from pain, or from finding comfort or sensual pleasures." The ECK Masters are hard workers in the physical body.

Those ECKists who are sincere about their spiritual unfoldment will discipline themselves with the Friday fasts.

Is fasting something an initiate should do simply because the Mahanta asks him to do it?

No one is forced to do anything in ECK, but more is expected of leaders. This is only for the spiritual benefit of the initiate—to help him reach Self- and God-Realization in the best way for him.

As you do the Friday fasts over a period of time, you will see an upward move in your thoughts and outlook toward life. You will get a greater control of your life than ever before.

Can my Friday fast help me become aware of living in the presence of God?

One of the fasts, the mental fast, is putting your attention on the Mahanta. This spiritual exercise finally becomes an exercise that's done moment to moment, all the time. You do this so that, eventually, you live every moment of your life in the presence of God. Every moment.

It's a good discipline. That's the purpose of the Friday fast.

If you do the disciplines—such as the spiritual exercises and the Friday fasts—I promise that life will open doors for everything you do.

The mental fast finally becomes an exercise that's done all the time. Eventually, you live every moment of your life in the presence of God. Every moment.

Workbook

The Friday Fast and You

1. What especially lit up for you in this chapter?

2. You can write a brief initiate report to the Master to ask him what kind of fast would be the most beneficial for you this Friday—and why. To begin, open your heart and sing your secret word as you go into contemplation. You can write your answer here.

3. Here are some spiritual gifts of unfoldment that the
    Friday fast offers (from "Help with Karma," pp. 72–79,
    and "More Gifts from the Friday Fasts," pp. 82–87).
    You can put a star by the ones that most appeal to you.

    ___ Lifts Soul above the social consciousness

    ___ Changes old mental structures and ideas

    ___ Develops inner discipline to reach God-
    Realization

    ___ Purifies your thoughts so they don't harm you

    ___ Helps pull you out of the karmic environment

    ___ Helps you develop the ability to handle prob-
    lems

    ___ Creates an upward move in your thoughts and
    outlook toward life

    ___ Allows you to get greater control of your life

    ___ Helps you remember experiences in the dream
    state

    ___ Makes it easy and natural to be in a high state
    of being every moment

    What other gifts have you noticed?

4. Want to express your gratitude for these gifts? You
   can write a thank-you note to the Master. Sing HU or
   your secret word for a few moments and just write
   from your heart. Then listen for a response from the
   Master—just for you.

   You can record your experience here.

5. Ask the Mahanta to reveal more to you about the
   benefits of the Friday fast. Take your request into contemplation. Then watch for the answers to come in
   your dreams, in daily life, or through the golden-
   tongued wisdom.

Want the Friday Fast to Be a Part of Your Life?

1. Each Friday you can review your list (workbook exercise 3 from "The Friday Fast and You," pp. 89–90) of gifts from the Friday fast before starting your day. At the end of the day, you can add more benefits to your list.

2. Each Friday ask the Mahanta, What kind of fast will be best for me to do today (singing my secret word, attention on the Master, etc.)? Ask, How will it help me spiritually? You can write your answer here.

3. If you'd like to get ideas for future Friday fasts, you can review what you wrote above.

4. Thursday night or Friday morning read a little from the Friday-fast chapter of *Karmabusters* and take it into light contemplation.

5. Friday morning ask the Mahanta for a cue or reminder to help you keep up the Friday fast today (e.g., when you walk through a doorway, when you have a negative thought, when you notice the sun shining).

6. Join a class on *Handbook for ECK Leaders* (for Second Initiates and above) or *Wisdom from the Master on Spiritual Leadership: ECK Leader's Guide* (for High Initiates). The Friday fast is part of the ongoing exercises covered in the class. You can also use the Friday-fast sheets on your own. They are found at the beginning of each chapter in *Handbook for ECK Leaders* and *Workbook for Wisdom from the Master on Spiritual Leadership*.

Karmabusters
Quick Reference Guide

Initiate Reports

The initiate report is for you. It is a love gift from the Mahanta, to help you clear the hurdles of life. The report is a privilege.

—*Karmabusters*, pp. 23–24

Who Writes Initiate Reports (*Karmabusters [KB]* pp. 6, 20)
- High Initiates
- Second, Third, and Fourth Initiates
- New chelas and First Initiates, if they wish

How Writing Initiate Reports Helps with Karma (*KB* pp. 5–8)
- Releases our burdens with the help of the Mahanta
- Gives a spiritual overview
- Shows our responsibility in a karmic matter

What to Write (*KB* pp. 6–7, 13–16)
- Spiritual experiences, Soul Travel and dream experiences
- Insights, thoughts, hopes, fears
- Problems, concerns
- Your spiritual progress—or areas to improve
- A plea for help or spiritual aid
- Your gratitude for the miracles of ECK, such as gifts of healing
- Insights into a recent ECK initiation

- What you have gained from an ECK discourse
- Spiritual—not administrative—topics

When to Write (*KB* pp. 5–7)
- Once a month
- The last day or the last Friday of the month are good.
- Whenever you feel it would be of benefit

Suggested Length (*KB* p. 16)
- Can just be a few lines
- It's better to keep it to one or two pages.

When to Mail Initiate Reports (*KB* pp. 7, 20, 25)
- Ask in contemplation.
- To share experiences or stories

Where to Mail Initiate Reports (*KB* pp. 20–21)
- Sri Harold Klemp, PO Box 2000, Chanhassen, MN 55317-2000 USA
- Mark envelope IRO (Initiate Report only) in lower left-hand corner.

Techniques for Writing Initiate Reports (*KB* pp. 14–15, 19)
- Write from the heart.
- List questions. A month later, review them. Report results.
- Review and condense experiences.
- Look for changes in yourself.

More Gifts from Writing Initiate Reports (*KB* pp. 6, 23–24)
- Helps you recall inner experiences from the month

- Helps you reach a better and more happy place in life
- Keeps your relationship with the Mahanta open and warm

Your Secret Word

Deep changes occur in you when you chant your word. Karma is dissolved from the lower bodies until the weight on Soul is lightened.

—*Karmabusters*, p. 39

How Chanting Your Secret Word Helps with Karma (*KB* pp. 35–40, 56)
- Increases your capacity to love
- Attunes you to the ECK
- Allows the Master to give you secret teachings and protection
- Helps control passions of the mind

Using Your Secret Word (*KB* pp. 39–45, 50, 57)
- Visualize it as a key to fit in a lock to open the door to the Light and Sound in the room beyond.
- Work with it, experiment, try different ways.
- Watch for subtle changes in attitude.
- Watch for direct experiences in the Light and Sound.
- Chant your word with another word.

How Long Your Secret Word May Last (*KB* pp. 47–50)
- Two weeks
- One initiation
- Two initiations
- An entire lifetime

When to Change Your Secret Word (*KB* pp. 47–50)

- If you feel it's not working.
- If you aren't remembering enough inner experiences (e.g., one a month).
- If you're ready to enter a new arena of consciousness.

Ways to Get a New Secret Word (*KB* pp. 50–53)

- Ask in contemplation.
- Watch your dreams.
- Try the Shariyat technique.
- Choose a word from the ECK works.

How Your Secret Word May Appear (*KB* pp. 35, 52)

- A symbol, picture, or everyday object
- An ordinary word
- A sound
- A word in an ECK book

More Gifts from Your Secret Word (*KB* pp. 42, 56–60)

- Uplifts Soul so that you can Soul Travel
- Builds inner strength
- Opens you to the full help of Divine Spirit
- Transforms you into a greater spiritual being

The Friday Fast

So what does a special day of fasting do?

It helps you develop the inner discipline to reach God-Realization. You learn the habit of being in ECK. Every moment. Every day.

—*Karmabusters*, p. 71

How the Friday Fast Helps with Karma *(KB* pp. 71–79)

- Lifts Soul above the social consciousness
- Changes old mental structures and ideas
- Develops inner discipline to reach God-Realization
- Purifies our thoughts so they don't harm us

Different Ways to Practice the Mental Fast *(KB* pp. 70–71, 79–82)

- Keep your thoughts upon the Mahanta all day long.
- Throw your negative thoughts into a mental trash can.
- Ask, "How would the Mahanta handle my problems today?"
- Sing HU or your secret word silently or out loud.
- Do everything that day in the name of the Mahanta.
- See the Mahanta in others.

More Gifts of the Friday Fast *(KB* pp. 72, 74, 82–87)

- Helps pull you out of the karmic environment
- Helps you develop the ability to handle problems
- Creates an upward move in your thoughts and outlook toward life
- Allows you to get greater control of your life
- Helps you remember experiences in the dream state
- Makes it easy and natural to be in a high state of being every moment.

Glossary

Words set in SMALL CAPS are defined elsewhere in this glossary.

ARAHATA. *ah-rah-HAH-tah* An experienced and qualified teacher of ECKANKAR classes.

CHELA. *CHEE-lah* A spiritual student. Often refers to a member of ECKANKAR.

ECK. *EHK* The Life Force, the Holy Spirit, or Audible Life Current which sustains all life.

ECKANKAR. *EHK-ahn-kahr* Religion of the Light and Sound of God. Also known as the Ancient Science of SOUL TRAVEL. A truly spiritual religion for the individual in modern times. The teachings provide a framework for anyone to explore their own spiritual experiences. Established by PAUL TWITCHELL, the modern-day founder, in 1965. The word means Co-worker with God.

ECK MASTER(S). Spiritual Masters who can assist and protect people in their spiritual studies and travels. The ECK Masters are from a long line of God-Realized SOULS who know the responsibility that goes with spiritual freedom.

GOD-REALIZATION. The state of God Consciousness. Complete and conscious awareness of God.

HU. *HYOO* The most ancient, secret name for God. The singing of the word *HU* is considered a love song to God. It can be sung aloud or silently to oneself.

INITIATION. Earned by a member of ECKANKAR through spiritual unfoldment and service to God. The initiation is a private ceremony in which the individual is linked to the Sound and Light of God.

KAL NIRANJAN, THE. *KAL nee-RAHN-jahn* The Kal; the negative power, also known as Satan or the devil.

99

KARMA, LAW OF.   The Law of Cause and Effect, action and reaction, justice, retribution, and reward, which applies to the lower or psychic worlds: the Physical, Astral, Causal, Mental, and Etheric Planes.

KLEMP, HAROLD.   The present MAHANTA, the LIVING ECK MASTER. SRI Harold Klemp became the Mahanta, the Living ECK Master in 1981. His spiritual name is WAH Z.

LIVING ECK MASTER.   The title of the spiritual leader of ECKANKAR. His duty is to lead SOUL back to God. The Living ECK Master can assist spiritual students physically as the Outer Master, in the dream state as the Dream Master, and in the spiritual worlds as the Inner Master.

MAHANTA.   *mah-HAHN-tah*   A title to describe the highest state of God Consciousness on earth, often embodied in the LIVING ECK MASTER. He is the Living Word. An expression of the Spirit of God that is always with you. Sometimes seen as a Blue Light or Blue Star or in the form of the Mahanta, the Living ECK Master.

MAHDIS.   *MAH-dees*   The initiate of the Fifth Circle (SOUL PLANE); often used as a generic term for all High Initiates in ECK.

PLANE(S).   The levels of existence, such as the Physical, Astral, Causal, Mental, Etheric, and SOUL Planes.

SATSANG.   *SAHT-sahng*   A class in which students of ECK study a monthly lesson from ECKANKAR.

SELF-REALIZATION.   SOUL recognition. The entering of SOUL into the Soul PLANE and there beholding Itself as pure Spirit. A state of seeing, knowing, and being.

SHARIYAT-KI-SUGMAD.   *SHAH-ree-aht-kee-SOOG-mahd*   The sacred scriptures of ECKANKAR. The scriptures are comprised of about twelve volumes in the spiritual worlds. The first two were transcribed from the inner PLANES by PAUL TWITCHELL, modern-day founder of ECKANKAR.

SOUL.   The True Self. The inner, most sacred part of each person. Soul exists before birth and lives on after the death of the physical body. As a spark of God, Soul can see, know, and perceive all things. It is the creative center of Its own world.

SOUL TRAVEL.   The expansion of consciousness. The ability of SOUL to transcend the physical body and travel into the spiritual worlds of God. Soul Travel is taught only by the LIVING ECK MASTER. It helps people unfold spiritually and can provide proof of the existence of God and life after death.

SOUND AND LIGHT OF ECK.   The Holy Spirit. The two aspects through which God appears in the lower worlds. People can experience them by looking and listening within themselves and through SOUL TRAVEL.

SPIRITUAL EXERCISES OF ECK.   The daily practice of certain techniques to get us in touch with the Light and Sound of God.

SRI.   *SREE*   A title of spiritual respect, similar to reverend or pastor, used for those who have attained the Kingdom of God. In ECKANKAR, it is reserved for the MAHANTA, the LIVING ECK MASTER.

SUGMAD.   *SOOG-mahd*   A sacred name for God. SUGMAD is neither masculine nor feminine; IT is the source of all life.

TEMPLE(S) OF GOLDEN WISDOM.   These Golden Wisdom Temples are spiritual temples which exist on the various PLANES—from the Physical to the Anami Lok; CHELAS of ECKANKAR are taken to the temples in the SOUL body to be educated in the divine knowledge; the different sections of the SHARIYAT-KI-SUGMAD, the sacred teachings of ECK, are kept at these temples.

TWITCHELL, PAUL.   An American ECK MASTER who brought the modern teachings of ECKANKAR to the world through his writings and lectures. His spiritual name is Peddar Zaskq.

VAIRAG.   *vie-RAHG*   Detachment.

WAH Z.   *WAH zee*   The spiritual name of SRI HAROLD KLEMP. It means the Secret Doctrine. It is his name in the spiritual worlds.

For more explanations of ECKANKAR terms, see *A Cosmic Sea of Words: The ECKANKAR Lexicon* by Harold Klemp.

For Further Reading and Study

Be the HU: How to Become a Co-worker with God
Harold Klemp

These talks by the Living ECK Master to ECK initiates of the Second Circle and above show how to become a Co-worker with God.

(For Second Initiates and above only)

Workbook for Be the HU
Harold Klemp

Read a chapter in *Be the HU: How to Become a Co-worker with God*, then enjoy the corresponding exercises in the workbook to help you recognize the Master's guidance in all aspects of your life.

(For Second Initiates and above only)

Ask the Master, Books 1 and 2
Harold Klemp

Sri Harold addresses some of life's toughest questions. He offers compassionate, straight-to-the-point, and sometimes surprising answers.

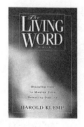

The Living Word, Books 1 and 2
Harold Klemp

The spiritual truth and divine love in Sri Harold's timeless articles from the *Mystic World* and *Eckankar Journal* show us how we can plan for and achieve tangible spiritual growth.

104

Wisdom of the Heart, Books 1 and 2
Harold Klemp

Nearly two decades of *Wisdom Notes*, letters from Sri Harold to the ECKists that appear in the *Mystic World*, teach new and practical ways to live the spiritual life to its fullest potential.

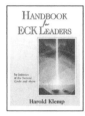

Handbook for ECK Leaders
Harold Klemp

Sri Harold is opening the door to your spiritual destiny through the secrets in this book. Use the exciting new format of an article by the Master followed by workbook exercises on that article to take his wisdom into your heart—and into daily practice.

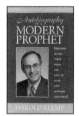

Autobiography of a Modern Prophet
Harold Klemp

Master your spiritual destiny. One man's journey illuminates the way. Venture to the outer reaches of the last great frontier, your spiritual destiny! The deeper you explore it, the closer you come to discovering your own divine nature as an infinite, eternal spark of God. This book leads you there.

The Shariyat-Ki-Sugmad, Books 1 and 2

The "Way of the Eternal." These writings are the scriptures of ECKANKAR. They speak to you directly and come alive in your heart.

Available through ECKANKAR. Call (952) 380-2222 or write to ECKANKAR, Dept. BK69, PO Box 2000, Chanhassen, MN 55317-2000 USA.

There May Be an
ECKANKAR Study Group near You

ECKANKAR offers a variety of local and international activities for the spiritual seeker. With hundreds of study groups worldwide, Eckankar is near you! Many areas have ECKANKAR centers where you can browse through the books in a quiet, unpressured environment, talk with others who share an interest in this ancient teaching, and attend beginning discussion classes on how to gain the attributes of Soul: wisdom, power, love, and freedom.

Around the world, ECKANKAR study groups offer special one-day or weekend seminars on the basic teachings of ECKANKAR. For membership information, visit the ECKANKAR Web site (www.Eckankar.org). For the location of the ECKANKAR center or study group nearest you, click on "Eckankar in Your Area" for a listing of those areas with Web sites. You're also welcome to check your phone book under **ECKANKAR**; call **(952) 380-2222, Ext. BK69;** or write **ECKANKAR, Att: Information, BK69, PO Box 2000, Chanhassen, MN 55317-2000 USA.**

☐ Please send me information on the nearest ECKANKAR center or study group in my area.

Please type or print clearly.

Name _____
         first (given)   last (family)

Street _____ Apt. # _____

City _____ State/Prov. _____

Zip/Postal Code _____ Country _____

About the Author

Harold Klemp was born in Wisconsin and grew up on a small farm. He attended a two-room country schoolhouse before going to high school at a religious boarding school in Milwaukee, Wisconsin.

After preministerial college in Milwaukee and Fort Wayne, Indiana, he enlisted in the U.S. Air Force. There he trained as a language specialist at Indiana University and a radio intercept operator at Goodfellow AFB, Texas. Then followed a two-year stint in Japan where he first encountered Eckankar.

In October 1981, he became the spiritual leader of Eckankar, Religion of the Light and Sound of God. His full title is Sri Harold Klemp, the Mahanta, the Living ECK Master. As the Living ECK Master, Harold Klemp is responsible for the continued evolution of the Eckankar teachings.

His mission is to help people find their way back to God in this life. Harold Klemp travels to ECK seminars in North America, Europe, and the South Pacific. He has also visited Africa and many countries throughout the world, meeting with spiritual seekers and giving inspirational talks. There are many videocassettes and audiocassettes of his public talks available.

In his talks and writings, Harold Klemp's sense of humor and practical approach to spirituality have helped many people around the world find truth in their lives and greater inner freedom, wisdom, and love.

International Who's Who of Intellectuals
Ninth Edition